Total Market Takeover®
For Roofing Contractors

Gordon Van Wechel

ISBN-10: 1722423935
ISBN-13: 978-1722423933

Second Edition

CONTENTS

Introduction to this Second Edition

When I published the first edition of Total Market Takeover® in 2014 it was not my intention to ever develop a second edition. My goal was to share the marketing strategies that we employed in our consulting with roofing contractors in a way that made it easier for others to implement them in their own businesses.

That is still the focus of this updated edition.

At the beginning of 2018 I sat with our Alchemy team to work on our company goals for the year. During the course of the discussion one of our team members commented on how different our work was now compared to when she joined the company just over two years earlier. As we continued our conversation together it became clear that she was right...many of our practices and services have changed in a relatively short period of time. Here are some examples:

- How we design the Home Page and About Us pages of new or updated websites
- Social media has become less important, but video more important
- A company's online reputation should be their top priority
- How the search engines, particularly Google, are increasing their emphasis on paid advertising

I'll address each of these challenges and the new strategies to meet them in the coming chapters.

Also new in this edition is a more detailed analysis of the five competitive forces that all of us as business owners struggle against to enhance our business profits. While it is rare in the roofing industry to compete against all five, every one of us faces two or three of them daily. How effective we are at meeting these challenges determines how profitable our company will be.

If you are one of those readers (like me) who skims through a book quickly to see if there is something I want to concentrate on, then I encourage you to focus on the final chapter on People Based Marketing. The strategies I introduce for In-Market and Site Visitor targeting are without a doubt the most significant change in how to generate new business since the office computer became affordable to all. In fact, I would go so far as to say that companies who do not embrace this new technology will lose significant market share over the next two years.

In the first edition of Total Market Takeover® I discussed the importance of we as business owners concentrating on innovating our companies. That has not changed. Somehow we have to find the time to step back from day to day operations and think ahead, embracing the changes that are inevitable.

My goal is that this new edition will help you do just that.

To Your Success!

Gordon

Introduction to the First Edition

When I was in graduate school one of my professors was fond of saying that whenever we read a book or listen to a speaker or read an article in an industry magazine one of the things we should always do is determine the authors bias. What is their frame of reference? Why do they reach conclusions they want you to accept? How did they choose the data they offer as proof of their position? Are they hoping to sell you something? Or convert you to a particular belief?

As you read this book I'm going to save you struggling with that issue and tell you right up front what I believe about marketing and the challenge of being a business owner in today's difficult economic climate. I wish I could claim it as original, but it is a statement I heard from the late Peter Drucker. He said, **"there are only two important activities for a business owner to be involved in: marketing and innovation. Everything else can be delegated."**

Marketing is sharing what your company does and inspiring people to do business with you. Innovation is making sure that your company is responsive to the changing wants of your customers and is the best that it can be. According to Professor Drucker these are the only activities that we as business owners should be focused on.

I understand how easy it seems for a university professor to make a statement like that. He's never worked 80 hour weeks, struggled to make payroll, and missed family activities to solve a customer service issue. Those of us who have been entrepreneurs know all too well about those times, particularly in the early days of starting our company.

Yet, I believe that Professor Drucker was right. As your business comes out of that initial "survival mode," as you identify some key people to help you and achieve a degree of stability, your focus as the owner must change if you are to create a sustainable enterprise. Most of us who have started a business have the vision that we are creating an asset that sometime in the future we can sell or turn over to a good manager and enjoy the fruits of our labor.

To make that happen we have to transition from working so hard "in" our business and begin to work "on" our business. That means we have to step back from making all the decisions and focus on innovating our company to be the best it can be, and then implement the most effective marketing strategies so customers can find us.

I've written this book to help you identify some of the best marketing strategies for a roofing business. These have been proven in "real world" situations with our clients in markets across the country. We call our program "Total Market Takeover®." That name evolved as we saw our clients begin to grow their market share as a result of implementing this multi-channel approach.

This is not a book about marketing theory. I'm going to share with you exactly what we do when implementing Total Market Takeover® for a roofing contractor. I encourage you, as you are reading, to take notes and put these strategies into practice. At the end of each chapter I'll suggest the next steps you should take if you want to implement that strategy into your business marketing plan. In the back of the book is some information about our company and a way to contact me directly. In fact, I'm offering readers a free one hour opportunity to talk with me about your business. I encourage you to do so.

To Your Success!

Gordon

Foundations: Know Your Business

When you think about growing your roofing company what comes to mind? Where is the best place to buy advertising? Should I open an office in another city? If I also offer windows and siding will that dilute my brand? I know I need to be online these days, but how do I do that?

All good questions. But they are the wrong questions!

Let me share an experience I had a few years ago after speaking at a marketing seminar in Denver. After my presentation I stayed around to talk with attendees and maybe find a client or two. As I was chatting with several people a man came up to the group and was obviously anxious to talk. As people drifted away he pulled me aside and blurted out, "I've signed a contract for a full page ad in the Yellow Pages for the next year and my ad is due tomorrow. How much will you charge me to write the ad?"

Without a pause I said, "$5,000."

"What!" he gasped. "Five grand just to write an ad for the yellow pages. That's crazy!"

"Really?" I said. "Think about it. I don't know you. I don't know your company and products you offer. I don't know your customer, your value proposition, or other advertising you do. If all you want is a list of platitudes and generalities to give the Yellow Pages rep you certainly don't need me. But if you want the $40,000 you're going to spend over the next year on that full page ad to actually give you a return on that investment, then I have to know all of those details about your business so I can write an ad that will attract the prospects you want."

I didn't get the job that day. (Interestingly enough, that same business owner called me several months later, asked for a meeting, and did hire our company to help them introduce a new product line.)

That experience is not unusual. In fact, far too often when I begin a conversation with a prospective client about marketing their roofing company they immediately want to talk tactics. "Do you think cable television is a good place to advertise? The local company is offering some great programs." My response to these questions is always the same: "it could be, we'll have to do the research before we can know for sure."

I'm going to say the same thing to you as you begin reading this book on marketing your roofing business. You were probably attracted by the title, Total Market Takeover®. That sounds pretty exciting, and while there are numerous marketing tactics that can work, they might not be the best for your company at this time with the marketing budget you have available.

In this opening chapter I'm going to share with you the conceptual foundation of Total Market Takeover®. I want you to feel confident that the information you're about to receive is credible, is accurate, and most importantly, will make you money. The bookstore shelves are full of books from people who are great at writing books, but short on experience when it comes to real-world results. I challenge you to go to your favorite bookstore and find more than 1 or 2 books that actually have useful advertising advice and examples that are of any relevance to you in your situation when trying to implement them into your roofing business. I know because I've spent hours at Barnes and Noble pouring over book after book in the sales, advertising, and marketing sections. I've scanned and read through hundreds of websites of so-called advertising experts. Through all that, I've only found a handful of what I would call an authoritative guide to getting results—that is, making real-world money—through marketing.

So I'll make you a few promises right now, right up front. First, I promise you that everything you will learn in this book will be applicable to you as the owner or executive in a roofing company. I promise you that you won't find yourself wondering, "what in the heck does that have to do with my business?" I promise you that all of the examples I share come from real-life, hands-on experience. I promise you if you will implement the strategies that I'm going to share you will see an immediate impact in the effectiveness of your marketing.

Or in other words, I promise you that this stuff will make you money. And that's the name of the game, right? I don't suppose you picked up a program on marketing for any other reason than to learn how to make more money, did you? Well, enough of the promises.

The title of this chapter is "Foundations," and in the next few pages I'm going to share with you four marketing concepts that form the bedrock of the Total Market Takeover® philosophy. They are:

- The Inside Reality of your company vs. the Outside Perception of the marketplace
- Strategic Marketing and Tactical Marketing
- Identifying your Ideal Customer
- Articulating your Value Proposition

I want to begin with these rather than jump ahead and show you how to design a Lead Generation Website or build an effective Pay Per Click campaign. We'll get to some tremendously powerful strategies for growing your company, but not until you understand why they can have such an impact.

Inside Reality vs. Outside Perception

There are really two different sides to your business. First, there's what I call the "Inside Reality" and second, the "Outside Perception." The Inside Reality has to do with all the things your business does that makes you valuable to your customers... from the roofing materials you use, your business operations, and the commitment to excellence of your management team. It's what gives you a competitive advantage in the marketplace.

The reason we call it the Inside *Reality* is because there's a good chance that the reality of what you do, and the customers' perceptions of what you do, aren't necessarily the same. You'll find that these two words— reality and perception—are very important to this process of winning the market share war for your business.

The Inside Reality encompasses everything you do and everything you are that makes you good. It's all your skills, your people, your expertise, your service to the customer—before, during, *and* after the sale—your systems, your operational procedures, your commitment to exceed customer expectations, your passion, and the way you conduct your business. Now you might think you're actually better than you are, or you might not be giving yourself enough credit for the things you do well. There is a reality of how valuable you are to the marketplace based on these things and others, both tangible and less tangible. That is what we call the Inside Reality.

If you asked your customers why they bought from you, they could tell you something quantifiable, specific, and instantly obvious. They could point to specific advantages of doing business with you and say, "That's why I had them replace my roof, that's why I refer my friends to them, that's why I'm a fan of the company." It's imperative that you begin to innovate your company so that there's a reason for people to choose you. But here's the problem: Just because you've achieved that level of innovation doesn't mean that customers are going to flock to your business. There's still a job of marketing that has to be done. And that's where the "Outside Perception" comes into play.

If the "Inside Reality" is about what you do and what you are that allows your business perform better, then the Outside Perception has to do with how customers and prospects perceive your industry and then your company. Invariably, the Inside Reality and the Outside Perception are different. Regardless of how good you are, or how good your "Inside Reality" is, your prospect is more than likely going to be apathetic. Not because they don't like you or they think your business is bad... it's because trying to figure out how good you are is the last thing on their priority list. Ask yourself this question: how many competitors, either direct or indirect, do you have in your business? Whatever that number is, that's how many choices your prospects have, and how many businesses they have to sift through to try to make a buying decision.

If you add a general perception about an industry that trends towards the negative, like the roofing industry, and the marketing battle for a company with an excellent Inside Reality is even more difficult. The problem is that most businesses don't have the ability to communicate via advertising and marketing their "Inside Reality" to the outside world. They can't lead prospects to the conclusion that they would have to be an absolute fool to do business with anyone else but you... even if they are good. That is the challenge of marketing your business, conveying the excellent Inside Reality of your company to a marketplace that tends to look at all roofing companies as basically the same.

The late business speaker Jim Rohn may have summed it up best in his lecture about communications. He was talking about personal communication, not business, but I think the principles are identical. He says to be a master communicator, all you've got to do is follow this simple three-step process: First, have something good to say. Second, say it well. And third, say it often. Does that make sense to you? Have something good to say, say it well, and say it often.

Having something good to say is the "Inside Reality" of your business, the excellent people and systems that you have created. The purpose of Total Market Takeover® is to improve the "Outside Perception" of your business, or in other words, how to say it well so people will choose you as their roofing contractor.

Sometimes when I share these concepts a business owner will say, "Yes, okay, that makes sense to me. The Inside Reality and the Outside Perception. But will these marketing strategies work for ME in MY business?" The answer is an unqualified "YES!" I work with companies in a variety of industries, and what I see is that on the most basic level all business owners want the exact same thing...more new customers, and less competition. They want to keep their margins, have their marketing and advertising work better, attract and retain more loyal customers, increase the conversion ratios for their sales people...and ultimately, they all want to make more money. True enough?

Now I want you to also recognize that all prospects and customers want the same things. They want the get the best deal, in terms of price and value. They want to feel confident that their money has been spent and their decision has been made to the best of their ability. You never hear anybody say, "I got bids from eight roofing companies and negotiated the best deals I could, and finally decided to buy where I got the third best deal." No! People instinctively want to make the best decision possible.

So we have two sets of values: The business wants more customers and loyal customers... and the customer wants the best possible deal, in terms of overall value. The process and principles that govern the matching of those two sets of values are exactly the same for every business. It's real simple: all you have to do as the business owner is give the prospect a reason to believe that you are actually the best deal, in terms of price and value, and then communicate those reasons to him in a way that he'll pay attention to and believe.

The problem is that most roofing companies come nowhere close to holding up their end of the bargain. Most have a tough time distinguishing and differentiating their business, and then communicating those advantages in an instantly obvious way. They can't make their "Outside Perception" match their "Inside Reality."

Think of it this way. What if you could find a way to drive in 20% more qualified leads into your business than you do right now... without increasing your monthly ad spend? Assuming you kept your same closing ratio, what would those 20% more qualified leads for the same money spent mean to your bottom line? And then consider this "what if". What if you could draw in 20% more qualified prospects, but you could ALSO find a way to increase your conversion ratio by 10%--across the board? What would THAT do to your bottom line? I'm going to go way out on a limb and say that you might be able to achieve those kinds of modest increases just by reading this book and implementing some of the marketing strategies I'm going to teach you.

Now that you understand the terms 'Inside Reality' and 'Outside Perception,' and the marketing challenge that is the result, I want to conduct a quick attitude check before moving on to the next subject. It doesn't really matter how your business is doing right now—whether it's growing, declining, or stagnant. Your attitude about winning in business and success is the most important thing if you are going to utilize the Total Market Takeover® program successfully. The attitude is: "I'm going to do whatever it takes, as long as it's legal, ethical, and moral, to make my business as innovative—and therefore valuable—as possible... and because of that I fully expect to win the lion's share of business... and I'll quite probably dominate all of my competitors in the process."

That is a bold statement, but you'll realize as you read along that this program isn't for business people who just want to get by, or who are looking for the marketing program of the month, or who just want to learn a bunch of tricks and techniques to shortcut success. If that's you, if you're satisfied with hanging out in the middle of the pack, then stop reading now because you will be frustrated and just waste your time.

Let me explain my point in another way. Right after he won his 5th MVP award, Michael Jordan said, "Hey, I'm not sitting around trying to figure out how to be the best player in the league. I'm continually trying to figure out how I can be the best I can be. Then the rest—the MVP awards and championships—will all fall into place."

The people who are successful implementing the Total Market Takeover® program I'm sharing are people who sincerely want to be the best they can be. People who have such a passion for their customers and doing things right that they'll do whatever it takes to get good enough to deserve all the business. This program is designed for people who can't stomach the thought of a customer doing business with another roofing company. You know, if you strive for that kind of excellence, you'll automatically surpass 90% of your competitors. They won't put in that kind of effort. They just won't and don't. It's up to you.

Hey, I feel that way. If you went to somebody else's marketing webinar, or read some other book on marketing, or, heaven forbid, hired another consulting firm to take your business to the next level, and I found out about it, I'd be ticked off! Not because I lost the business and the chance to make money, but because I know that there's not another book, seminar, workshop, or consultant—anywhere, at any price—that will give you the results that I can. There are very few consultants out there who have almost 40 years of active, hands on experience growing businesses of their own, and who built three national companies in the process. Since 2003 I've worked as a consultant with dozens of other business owners in a variety of industries and professional practices helping them to reach their goals.

That might sound strong, but I would hope you feel that way about your business. I would hope that you would put that kind of effort into perfecting your craft so that it's worthy of the lion's share of the dollars in your market area. If you don't feel that way, and you're not willing to put in that kind of effort, then throw this book away right now and get ready to get clobbered by someone who does feel that way. I guarantee you they're out there. Remember I said that with the right mindset you'd pass up 90% of your competitors? Well, there's ten percent left out there that are trying to dominate the market, and it's going to be a dogfight. To think otherwise would be naïve.

Strategic Marketing and Tactical Marketing

The second foundation principle I want you to understand in the distinction between Strategic and Tactical marketing. This is important because you want to focus your time where it is most effective. Most roofing contractors concentrate on Tactical marketing; I want to encourage you to give your attention to Strategic marketing. Let me begin by defining what those terms mean.

Strategic marketing is what you say, how you say it, and who you say it to. Tactical marketing is where you say it. Let me say it in a different way: Strategic marketing is your marketing plan, it is how you define and identify your ideal customer, the target market that you are selling to, and the things that you are going to say that are specifically relevant to those people. Tactical marketing is how you are going to find them. That might mean radio advertising, or changing your website, possibly putting a display ad in the newspaper--that's the tactical side.

I know from experience with a lot of business owners that you spend most of your time on the tactical. Here's an example. You decide to run a seasonal promotion, which means you will need to put a display ad into the local newspaper. Immediately you put together some ideas for the ad, then call the salesperson at the newspaper to help you with layout. They are more than happy to take your money and put your ad in for the weekend. By the middle of the next week you are scratching your head and wondering why the phone hasn't been ringing.

Has that ever been your experience?

Here's why. We spend our time on tactical marketing (where to say it), when what we really want to be doing is stepping back and focusing on the strategic side (what you say, how you say it, and who you say it to.) One of the people that I learn marketing from years ago had a phrase I want to share that with you. What he used to say was, "if you want to know what John Smith buys, you have to see the world through John Smiths eyes." Here is what he meant. As a business owner you must understand what is important to your customer, the "conversation going on in their minds," so that you can address their desires.

Instead, here is what most of us do. We know our product and service really well, we know our company and how good we are, so that's the frame of reference that we use in our marketing. We write ads that makes sense to us, that have a lot of "features" without paying

15

attention to the "benefits" our customer is actually looking for. This is why you see so many ads with ludicrous platitudes saying things like, "we are the best," "in business for 39 years," "we do quality work," and "our staff is friendly." Are statements like these of any value to a prospect who is deciding whether to sign a contract with your roofing company or a competitor?

So as a business owner, how do you know how John Smith sees the world? How do you know what John Smith's eyes are looking for? Simple, you ask John. When we work with a client we get a list of recent customers and, with the customers permission, interview them asking a series of fourteen question designed to help us uncover their real motivations. Let me offer three of the most important and encourage you to have some conversations with recent roofing customers.

1. Under what circumstances does the typical prospect begin to think about having a new roof installed? Sometimes this is obvious, like when there has been a hailstorm and many homes are damaged. But what about the person who is thinking about selling their home in a year and wants to see if the roof is intact enough to get through the sales and inspection process? Or the homeowner who isn't thinking of moving, in fact, the opposite. They want to talk with you about different roofing materials and are looking at long term value and aesthetic considerations. Each one of these prospects has a different motivation, and it will take a unique marketing message to reach them.

2. What things are important to your prospects when buying a new roof. Again, the simple answer might be price and/or materials. Also think about the buying process, what is important to your prospects when they go through the process of getting a new roof? What are steps in the process that might be challenging for your customers? Since they don't buy a new roof very often, just knowing the right questions to ask is a challenge. Think about what your customers want, *as well as what they want to avoid*. In your marketing you want to address all of those issues, both factual and experiential.

3. What are the relevant and important issues that a prospects need to be aware of when making a decision about a new roof. What are the challenges that John and Jane Smith are having as they come into your world, and what can you do to innovate your company to address those challenges in a way that is comfortable for the Smiths?

All three of these questions are Strategic, that is, they focus on John Smith's desires, his "hot buttons." I recognize that hot button is kind of an old school term, today you might think of it as what are the keywords a prospective roofing customer would use when they search on Google for a contractor. Don't assume that you know the answer to that question. Even for a task as simple as finding a roofing contractor people will use a variety of search terms.

4. Where did you look for a roofing company? That is, how did you find us and call for information? This question is Tactical. Once you know where most of your customers are looking, and the search terms they are using, you'll know where to invest your marketing budget for the highest return.

Identifying Your Ideal Customer

This may seem obvious, and you may be saying to yourself, "my ideal customer is someone who needs a new roof." I agree, but by just generalizing your customer to be anyone who needs a new roof you force yourself into spending your marketing budget advertising for leads. That means you are using multi-media like radio and television, "leads" companies like Home Advisors and others, hiring canvassers to go door to door in neighborhoods, and other generic lead generation activities. I know that is what most roofing companies do the create new business, but what if there was a more effective way? Not only more effective, but a marketing plan that allowed you to calculate the actual return on investment for your monthly spend?

Well there is. In fact, this book is going to help you focus on specific strategies to maximize the impact of your advertising dollars. Let me first explain the difference between a defined and non-defined market, then give you a technique for identifying who your ideal customer really is.

A defined market place is one where you can identify, pinpoint, and you can obtain a list of people that are prospects for your roofing company. A non-defined market is just the opposite, you have to go out and advertise to create leads to begin the marketing process.

The more you can define your market place, the more effective your marketing is going to be, and the more profitable your business is going to be. I don't know if he originated the statement, but Dan Kennedy was the person I heard say "if everybody is your market, then nobody is your market." If you stop and think about that for a minute makes sense. If you are out there trying to sell a new roof to anyone and everyone in your city you have a tough challenge. To the extent that you can narrow that market down and identify specific people or groups who are potential targets it makes your marketing that much more effective. How do you do that? Here are several ideas:

1. What services do you offer? Do you only do roof replacement, or do you also offer repair services? Is roofing your only business, or do you have another related product or service (like siding and windows, concrete flatwork, gutter install, etc.) Do you have a completely different business during the winter? Start the ideal customer identification process by first segmenting the different businesses you have. Each one has one or more ideal customers you can specifically identify and market to.

2. Think about the demographics in your market area. What part(s) of town are you currently getting most of your business from? Is that where you really want to be? Are their neighborhoods or surrounding communities that you would like to have more jobs in? Are you typically getting $10,000 replacement jobs when there are neighborhoods in your city that would have $18,000 or $20,000 jobs?

3. As you begin to think about your ideal customer, where do they gather in the greatest numbers? What other businesses or organizations transact business with them? How can you obtain or build a list using their other involvements?

4. How do they like to be communicated with? What do they read? Listen to?

The easiest way to begin to identify your ideal customer is to take a look at the customers you have done business with in the past year. Here are some questions to ask about them:

- Who made the decision? What is their gender, age, income, occupation?
- Where, exactly, did they live? (get a map of your area and use pushpins to locate every customer's address.)
- How did they hear about you? How did they contact you? Or did you make the initial contact with them?
- Why did they buy from you rather than a competitor? Be honest with yourself here. If you are willing to discount your price to get the job then recognize that fact.
- What, if any, continuing contact have you had with the customer since finishing their job?

Now, what do you do with this data? First, you should be able to quantify some information about your company and the success of your marketing efforts as a result of doing this analysis.

As you look at the customer profile that emerges ask yourself if that is the who you want to continue to market to? If so, then you're going to be pleased with the strategies I'll be sharing with you in the coming chapters. They will help you target your ideal customers more accurately and at a lower cost than much of what you are doing today.

If not, if you want to grow your business with a different level of customer, then I'm going to show you how to do that. Here's a quick example. We worked with a contractor who had a good size business in many of the middle class neighborhoods on the West side of his city. He asked if we could help him break into some of the suburbs on the South side where most of the executive homes were located. After analyzing the market we designed campaigns using online banner ads focused on the geographical area he wanted to generate business in. We were able to place his ad in front of homeowners in those neighborhoods as they went online. The cost was very reasonable, less than $5.00 for a thousand impressions! Within a few weeks he began to get calls from the South side. The profit from his first job paid his entire marketing budget for the year!

Do you do any commercial work? It is an easy matter to get a list of the owners of buildings that fit the profile of work you want to do. Even easier to identify the property management companies who work with building owners. One of our clients decided to market to owners of small apartment properties, 12 units or less. He was able to get a list of the building owners from a title company (through a Realtor friend). He also identified several property management companies who worked with these owners. In his case about 20% of the owners did not live in the area and were grateful to have a licensed professional monitoring the condition of the roofs of their investments.

He contacted each owner and management company with an offer of a free roof inspection. His follow up offer was for an annual maintenance contract "to extend the life of their roof." He set up a program of contacting these building owners four times each year with this offer. Over time he had more than twenty buildings "under contract" at between $400 and $900 a year for inspections every six months. His total cost for the marketing plan was less than $1000 for the year! Oh, and every time one of these roofs needed to be replaced guess who got the business without having to bid against other contractors? That's right, our client.

Were the inspections every six months a problem? No. On a week when he had a crew that finished a job early, or the occasional slow week, he'd send a crew to inspect using the checklist he'd developed. They would take photos using their cell phones. He would then take the information and pictures and prepare a short report for the building owner and manager. In fact, his office manager did the reports and sent them out for him! All he did was read and sign.

Another way to identify a subset of property owners is to join investor groups. In every major city there are groups of single family home investors, many of whom buy distress properties to fix up and hold or "flip" as soon as possible. Many of these groups meet once a month for lunch. For an investment of 2 hours a month of your time as well as some follow up marketing with a good offer, and you could be the "go to" roofer for these investors. What is that worth if you were able to capture ten jobs a year? A good place to find these groups is to go to www.meetup.com.

What I'm suggesting you do is consider how many "market niches" you can identify in your local area. The more you can focus your marketing on these smaller groups the higher your return on monthly ad spend.

In the final chapter I'm going to introduce you to "People Based Marketing," an innovation that is just now becoming available to contractors who qualify.

Articulating Your Value Proposition

The final piece to your well constructed marketing foundation is to define your value proposition. That is, "why should a prospect choose your roofing company instead of your competitors?" One of the reasons I suggested you spend time identifying your ideal customer(s) is because it is very likely that you will have a different value proposition for each customer. The value proposition should answer the questions: "Why should I buy *this* product or service?" as well as "Why should I do anything at all". It is a clear and specific statement about the tangible benefits of your offer and should be stated in terms understood and accepted by the target customer.

First I'll suggest a way to think through and write out your value proposition, then give you some examples for different customers. The first portion of the value proposition asserts the value of the offering in terms of the results and benefits, and it demonstrates how you are equipped to deliver that value (it notes your skills and abilities). The second sentence asserts the positioning of that value by establishing a contrast.

First Sentence:

- Because we have *(skills, experience, knowledge or other attribute)*
- We are able to *(provide service, fix the problem, or other deliverable)*
- This means *(benefits the client will value)*
- For *(the client)*

Second (optional) Sentence:

- Unlike *(primary competitive alternative),*
- Our service *(statement of primary differentiation).*

Here are some examples:

First, for a homeowner in a mid-range neighborhood who has suffered storm damage:

"Because we have superior materials buying power made possible by the number of jobs we do each year, we are able to offer you top quality 30 year roofing shingles at the same price as the lower quality 20 year. This means that you will have a better, longer lasting roof and we'll be able to complete the job using the funds allocated by your insurance company without you paying anything out of your pocket other than your deductible."

Second, a property investor:

"Because we have superior materials buying power made possible by the number of jobs we do each year, we can replace the roof less expensively and get materials delivered to the site within 48 hours. This means the job will be done quickly and at a lower cost, enabling you to flip the property at a higher margin."

Third, homeowner in a higher end neighborhood:

"As a market leader here in (your town), we enjoy superior buying power made possible by the number of jobs we do each year. This enables us to offer you the best possible materials for your job, in a variety of finishes and colors to enhance the street appeal of your home. Our crews have experience in the finish details around skylights, chimneys, and vents so you can rely on the quality of the workmanship. This means you will have a better, longer lasting roof, with the job completed on time."

I hope you are beginning to see the importance of a clear value proposition tailored to each type of customer you work with. A value proposition cannot be a series of platitudes and generalities. It must draw a line in the sand between you and your competitors, and clearly state the benefit to the customer of working with your company.

WHAT TO DO NOW:

1. Identify at least three different groups of customers you would like to market your company to. They might be in different neighborhoods or types of buildings or prospects for various services you offer. Don't just name them, "residents in Holly Hills." Really think about who the residents of Holly Hills are. Write out a description of the typical resident. Are they married couples? How many kids? What do they drive? Where do they shop? What size are their homes? How old are the homes (roofs)? What kind of jobs do they have?

The reason this is such an important exercise is that when you begin to design your marketing plan, knowing specifically who you are marketing to will help you determine what to say and how to say it (Strategic marketing.)

2. Develop a value proposition for each of your ideal customers. Concentrate on the benefits to the customer and what makes you different from the other roofing companies who might make them an offer.

This is important because it is your value propositions that will form the basis of the advertising that you write. Whether it is a radio spot, pay per click ad, or direct mail piece it must focus on the value you bring to the prospect.

That is why I titled this chapter "Foundations." These activities are the foundation of an effective and profitable marketing strategy for your company.

Reputation Marketing--Your Business is "In The Stars"

I am not exaggerating when I say that controlling and marketing your reputation online has become, in the last two years, the single most critical aspect of any online marketing you do for your company. This task is completely different from the Search Engine Optimization or Social Media Marketing that is the mainstream, and that you have a lot of companies calling every week and offering to do for you. The reality is that the strategy for online marketing of your roofing business forever changed in September of 2014. Did you know that?

That is because in August, 2014, the search engines dramatically changed their algorithm for ranking websites on their pages. This wasn't just Google; Bing and Yahoo agreed and rewrote their programs at the same time. Here is the major change. Prior to that time where your site appeared on the page was the result of a complicated calculation that included several variables, but was most heavily weighted by the number of "backlinks" connected to your site. Without going into a lot of tech-speak let me say that it was a relatively simple matter for those of us in the Search Engine Optimization business to artificially manufacture these backlinks. Which meant that we could take a website and drive it to the first pages of the search engines using technology without regard to how many people might actually be looking for or finding value on the website.

The fundamental change that was implemented is replacing backlinks as a primary criteria for page rank with your company reputation, as defined by actual customers who have used your service and then posted a review of their experience on line. The search engines are now sending their spiders through dozens of "review sites" looking for comments about your roofing company. When they find one, it is harvested and combined with other reviews in a formula that results in a "Star Rating" for your business. One star is bad, five stars is the best.

This is a game changer in how you market your company online. In this chapter I want to share with you what you can do to get and stay ahead of the reputation wave. It is a fact that the roofing industry does not react quickly to changes in the marketing world. That's good news for you reading this chapter--you can be the market leader in your area. Here's what we're going to talk about:

- Specific game changers and how they impact your business
- What your prospects are looking for today in choosing a roofing contractor
- What is "Reputation Marketing"
- Strategies to make your company the reputation market leader
- Some questions about Reputation Marketing we often hear

Before I share those ideas with you, let me ask a question. I'm sure you realize that every day people go online searching for a product or service vendor. But do you know just how many people are searching? You might be surprised. At the time I'm writing this, June 2018, I asked one of our support team members to do a quick analysis of how many people searched for a roofing contractor in several cities around the country. This is the number of people who search *each month*, on average, in each of these cities:

Phoenix, AZ	3118
Miami, FL	3670
Charlotte, NC	1568
Portland, OR	1847
Des Moines, IA	948
Columbus, OH	2983
Pittsburg, PA	2106

Just imagine hundreds if not thousands of people online every single month looking for your business. The question is, can they find you? Every day people in your community are looking for a roofing contractor. As they do so, they are asking themselves this question: "who should I do business with? Who can I trust?" What they're doing is looking for the most reputable company. In this chapter I'm going to show you how to make sure that you are the business that they call, and not your competition.

Here's another question for you. Think about your own process when you are looking for a specific product or service. Would you buy from a company that has bad ratings and reviews? Obviously you wouldn't. But let me suggest a more realistic way to think about that question.

Three companies are, for all practical purposes, identical. All three have what you are looking for, and the price point is the same. One has six good reviews; the other has four good reviews but one bad. And the third has no reviews at all. Which one do you buy from? Almost everyone would say the company with six good reviews. Now why is that? Because we want to have a great buying experience too. We're looking to see that a company is consistent in delivering that experience or that product or service that we want to buy.

This is exactly what prospects looking for a roofing contractor do every single day. They go online and search to find the most reputable company to do business with. Only one bad review can send the customer from your website or your listing online to someone else's. That means the difference between your phone ringing or your competition's phone ringing.

Game Changers That Affect Your Company Today

Game Changer Number One. When you do a search for any company name and their city, the resulting listing reveals the company's reputation. Here is an example for a roofing company in Columbus, OH.

Acme Roofing & Siding - Contractor | Columbus, OH
acmeroofingandsiding.com/ ▾
Family owned/operated. Warranties available. BBB member. Residential and commercial work. Roofing, siding, windows, more. Call 614-477-7663.
4.4 ★ ★ ★ ★ ✦ 12 Google reviews · Write a review · Google+ page

I entered in the name of the company plus their city. As you can see what comes up is their listing in Google. But look at the bottom line of the listing: their reputation score. In this case, we see that Acme Roofing & Siding has a score of 4.4 based on twelve reviews. They have an excellent score, and have done a good job of inviting their customers to give them a review. By the way, this is not one of our clients, I just randomly chose Acme to use as an example.

Here's why this game changer is so important: anyone searching for a roofing company listing, even just for directions or to get the phone number, is going to see their reputation. This is done automatically by the search engines, as a business you have no control over your reputation being shown. Consider the situation where someone recommends your company to a friend. According to both Real Strategic and Bright Local there is an 87% probability that the person will look up your company online...maybe just to get the phone number. If you have a poor review score, what are the chances they are going to call you? Even though they were referred, in the past almost a guarantee that you'd get an opportunity to bid for that business, if your reputation score is less than 4 stars they will probably go elsewhere.

Ask yourself this question: when someone types in your roofing company name, what will they find? What is your reputation score? Does it show no reviews at all, or some good and others not so good?

Game Changer Number Two. Customer reviews are now a major factor in almost every type of online marketing, and this is all done automatically. Your reviews, good and bad, show up in Google maps, your Google plus listing. (Same for the other search engines.) Your star rating is included in your Pay Per Click ads. They show up on organic website listings. They show up in local directories like Yelp and City Search and Bing and Yahoo, in the online Yellow Pages. Reviews are now a major factor in almost every type of online marketing. Like it or not, everyone searching for your company or in your category will see them.

Which leads us to game changer number three: and that's the reality that SEO, social media, Pay Per Click, local marketing--all of the strategies we've done on line for the past five or more years-- none of it is as effective anymore if you have bad reviews or a bad reputation online.

I want you to think carefully about what I'm going to write next-- especially those of you who have done it yourself or paid someone to do online marketing for you. Maybe you're still paying. Why would you want to do all that work, spend all the time and money getting to the top of the search engines, and then when people find you they see bad reviews? You've just wasted your resources!

What we've done in our firm over the last 24 months is a complete flip-flop in our online marketing strategy. Before we used to start with Google maps, we'd do Yelp and video marketing. We do blogging, social media, and press releases, our tech people would create link wheels all designed to help our clients get to the first page for their primary keywords. That's completely the opposite of what today's marketing is about.

Step one if you want to be effective in marketing on line today is you need to create a five-star reputation first. Then you market your products and services online. Because your phone is not going ring if you don't have that five-star reputation that your prospects are looking for.

What Your Prospects Are Looking For Today in Choosing a Roofing Contractor

OK, let's change it up a little. I've been pretty negative about the impact reputation has made, but there are some really some positive game changers that are a result of this emphasis on reputation.

Game Changer Number Four. Reviews send you prequalified, presold customers; the reason is because buyers trust reviews as much as personal recommendations. So reviews can be incredibly bad for you if they're bad. But they can be incredibly good for you if they're really good. According to independent studies conducted by two international marketing agencies, Bright Local and Local Marketing Genius, 87% of people who are referred to a business will first go online and look up the company's reputation. That is almost 9 out of every 10 prospects!

Now, stop for a minute and think about growing your company. Would you rather create a marketing plan that focused on people that don't know you, don't like you, don't trust you, and always are worried about price? Or would you rather create a marketing plan that attracts people that feel they know you, people that already like you, people that trust you and act like they are all referrals?

Of course you want the later, you want to create a referral based marketing plan. Well, for the first time ever, our online marketing can be just as powerful as referral marketing. Why, Because nine out of ten people trust reviews just as much as personal recommendations!

So we need those five star reviews on your website and on your listings. That's as good as someone's mother saying you should get your roof from this company. That's as good as someone's best friend saying, you know what, you should call ABC Roofing, I used them and they were amazing. Having positive reviews is just as good as a colleague at work saying look, if you need a new roof you should go to this business. They do a great job. You can think of it that way because seventy two percent of buyers trust reviews just as much as personal recommendations.

Reviews are powerful marketing that you need for your business.

The A. E. Neilson company recently did a survey of "marketing media trust" that polled tens of thousands of people here in the United States. They offered a list of both on and offline media and asked whether the survey respondents trust that media as they are investigating a product or service provider. The results were startling.

Television ads came in at 47%, email marketing 40%, even your website content only averaged 58%. A newspaper article written about your company is trusted 62% of the time. Online reviews from a complete stranger: 82%!

If you're not yet convinced why having a 5 star reputation is so vital to business let me share just one more statistic with you. Consumers look up an average of 10 reviews before making a decision. What does this mean for your business?   First, all these consumers are online. They're looking for reviews. Second, and more important, they're looking at multiple reviews, not just one or two.

For those of you that have been wondering to yourself how many reviews is enough, here's your answer.   Seventy percent of consumers trust a business with a minimum of 6-10 reviews. So a minimum target you want to set for your roofing business is ten 5-star reviews.

The reality of the marketplace today is that you are not credible without five-star reviews. Without a five-star reputation and a minimum of ten reviews, your business just can't be trusted when people actually find you. This is the difference between your phone ringing and it not ringing. More importantly, this the difference   between   your   phone   not   ringing   and   your competition's phone ringing.

So what exactly is Reputation Marketing?

Well, it's very simple. Positioning your company as the market leader in front of thousands of buyers with a five-star reputation. It's building a five-star reputation online and then going out and marketing that reputation. As we just learned, this is the most powerful and trusted type of marketing you can do to grow your roofing company in today's market.

OK, enough background...let's get to the bottom line. How do you create a reputation marketing program for your roofing business? I know this is why you're here, so let me give you the step-by-step strategies.

What is your online reputation today?

The first step is to really understand your current reputation. So let me ask you. Do you know you reputation online? Do you know what people are saying about you right now? If you don't, the first step is to open a new browser window and go to Google. Then type in your business name, not with the www, just your business name. Click enter.

The results page will start with paid ads if you are using Adwords in your marketing, then in most cases you'll see a link to your website followed by several links to individual pages within your website.

What I want you to look at is on the right side of the page, Google offers a more complete listing of your business. This is your "Google My Business" listing. If you have properly claimed this listing it will include photos you have uploaded as well as accurate information on your business hours and address. There will also be a link someone can click on to go to your website and another link to get directions to your place of business.

Most important, right under your business name, is a summary of your review star rating and a clickable link so someone can go read those reviews. Here is an example of what a potential customer will see when looking up your company (I've blocked the company name):

3.7 ★★★★ ★ 41 Google reviews

Website   Directions

Roofing contractor in Albuquerque, New Mexico

Address:

Hours: Open · Closes 5PM ▾

Phone: (505) 884-0662

Suggest an edit

on Google

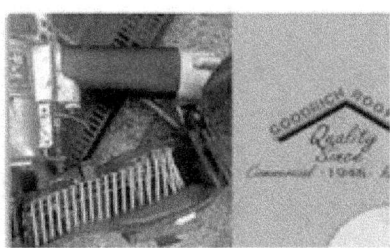

As you can see, this company has a total at this time of 41 reviews that have been posted on Google. This is excellent. Their overall "Star Rating" on a scale of 5 is just 3.7. That is not so good. In general, people are looking for a company with at least a four star reputation. Having a few reviews that are three stars or less isn't the end of the world, in fact, it makes your overall rating more believable. Prospects understand that sometimes a customer will not be satisfied and reflect that in their review. But if the overall majority of reviews are positive, and you have enough reviews to demonstrate you are consistently asking for them, those who are looking for a contractor will consider your company.

Also notice that this is 'clickable' link, prospects can click on it and go read the reviews that Google has collected.

Reputation Rules Update

Starting in 2017, the search engines began implementing some significant changes to their algorithms concerning how reviews are gathered and credited to your business. While these updates were to be fully put into operation by the end of that year, at the time I'm writing this, June 2018, we can see that they still have not been rolled out in all categories. Here the four most significant of the new rules.

1. All reviews must have a minimum of 30 characters or they will not be included in your star rating calculation. The search engines are looking for a couple of sentences from your customers describing their experience. Giving a five star rating with no comment, or just a couple of words will no longer be accepted.

2. Reviews older than 24 months will no longer be considered. This means that every month all reviews that are two years old "drop out" of your star rating. Google wants to be sure that your prospects are seeing reviews that reflect your current level of service.

3. Companies with a new star rating of less than 4.0 will be

penalized in search results. That means that your website will not be presented to someone searching for a roofing contractor as frequently if your net score is not at least 4.0.

To put that in perspective, the average star rating for all companies in all business niches in the United States is 4.16. In essence, Google is asking that you are "almost average" to maintain your status in the search engine results pages. If your rating is less than 4.0 it doesn't mean your site will not be offered when a prospect is searching for a contractor, but it will not be shown as frequently.

4. "Anonymous" reviews will no longer be posted. That is, reviews from "a Google user" that used to be allowed have now been deleted by the Google. Every review must be 'signed' by the reviewer.

Building Your 5-Star Reputation

I hope that I have conveyed the importance of achieving an excellent online reputation as defined by your Star Rating with the search engines. If you have never focused on developing your online reputation, how do you do it? Here are some steps to consider:

First, your staff needs to be made aware of the important role each of them play in building your company reputation. You will want to create a reputation marketing culture in your company. It's not enough to try to fix things after the fact, you want to be proactive inside your business to make sure that every single person in your company is on the same page when it comes to service standards.

Ongoing management of your reputation is not a "one and done" processes, you want to continue to keep your 5-star reputation going. In reality you're only one customer away from a bad review. Think about it, everybody has a bad day: the receptionist, your sales person, one of the guys out on a crew, even you. Every one of our businesses is just one day and just one customer away from a bad review. So we want to keep our eyes on the ball, to make sure we stay focused.

Second, where do you want your reviews to be found? There are literally hundreds of sites where a customer can leave a comment about your company, how do you prioritize them? Simple, just one word: Google.

For a contractor in the roofing industry the most important place to ask a customer to leave a review is on your Google My Business page. This is where prospects will be searching, make it easy for them to find you.

(By the way, this is not true for all industries. Restaurants are best served building their reputation on Yelp, hospitality industry companies on Trip Advisor, and medical practices can choose from a wide variety of specialty sites.)

If you have not yet "claimed" your Google My Business page make this a high priority. Go to this link and click the "Start Now" button: business.google.com.

Third, make it easy for your customers to leave a review. We like to provide our clients with a simple business card that has an invitation to leave a review and gives them the link they'll need to get to your Google My Business or other location where you would like them to review you.

The best time to invite someone to leave a review is at the end of the job when you doing the final walk-through. If you wait just a couple of days and send them an email invitation the percentage of people who will actually follow through and leave a review drops significantly.

By handing them a card with directions, personally asking for a positive review, and sharing how important this is for your business, many people will take the time to leave a review.

Fourth, consider a third party review collection and display program. Did you know there are several software programs that have been developed specifically to request and post reviews? These are usually available only through advertising agencies or search engine optimization companies. If you have a marketing company working on your behalf, ask them about this. Several of the leading products that are available include:

Reputation Aegis (this is the program we currently offer our clients.)
Reputation Loop
Reputation Kahuna
Reputation Defender
Vendasta
Webimax
Nearby Now

Another benefit of these programs is that they will monitor a wide variety of online review sites on a daily basis and "pull" these reviews into your review page.

If you decide to employ an agency to help you develop and maintain your online reputation be sure they are compliant with the latest Google updates I mentioned earlier. Many of these software programs offered an "internal loop" that diverted a negative review, generally defined as 3 stars of less, to a different page that did not allow the reviewer to forward their review to the internet. Instead, it 'captured' that review and sent it to the business owner for their response. *This strategy has been specifically prohibited by the new search engine guidelines.* Do not make the mistake of engaging one of these services, you could see your website severely penalized.

Fifth, the testimonials you have on your website are not included in your overall star rating by the search engines. In fact, they are not indexed at all. Since they cannot be sourced to an IP address that is independent from your website the search engine spiders ignore them completely.

Related to this is an important fact. Frequently I'll be asked, "why can't I just have several of my employees type these old testimonials into the Google page and have them used?" The simple answer is that Google tracks the individual computer address (its IP address) that is the source of the review. If multiple reviews are submitted for the same company from that unique address they will all be ignored.

How can you include your good reviews on your website? Several of the third party review companies have a way to add their review collection page to your website. Your web master can add an item into the menu bar for reviews and paste the code for the review page into your site. One of the reasons we use the Reputation Aegis program for our clients is the ease of doing this.

Sixth, you'll also want to post your 5-star reviews on the social media sites you belong to. With all of the talk about social media in the last couple of years, for many companies it has been a disappointment as far as generating new business. That all changes when you're using reputation marketing in your social media. When 5 star reviews are being posted several times each week to your Facebook, Instagram, LinkedIn and other pages they become a powerful source of leads.

Seven, do you have sales people in your company? It doesn't matter if they work on site or off, when you arm them with marketing pieces featuring your 5-star reviews their closing rates will go up dramatically. Imagine the ability to sit in front of a prospect that's on the fence about whether they should go with you or buy from a competitor. Then you say, "don't take my word for it. Let's go online and see what other customers just like you experienced, and what they thought about working with us." Then you read all your five-star reviews in front of them.

You should also provide each salesperson with a hard copy of the reviews in a notebook to show a prospect that might not have a computer handy. You can also use an iPad or Android pad, as most people will have wireless in their homes. Remember, statistically speaking, having those reviews is just as powerful as having their best friend or family member, a colleague at work recommending your roofing company to that customer. So you're going to be able to close a lot more sales if you arm yourself with reputation marketing.

Some Questions About Reputation Marketing

One that comes up a lot. "I have had someone leave a bad review on Yelp, how can I delete it?"

The short answer is that you can't. I know that there are

companies out there who promise to eliminate past bad reviews, but the truth is it's just not possible. The only real solution is to focus on generating as many 4 and 5 star reviews as you can, as quickly as possible. Most all of the sites display reviews in order of most recent first. So over a few months you will be able to "push down" the bad review so not as many people see it.

There is also an "aging" component to the calculation used to determine your star rating. The most recent reviews are given a greater emphasis by the review sites that aggregate reviews and apply a rating number.

The only exception to this is your Facebook business page. If someone says something negative there, you or your page administrator can delete the conversation. The challenge is that you have to monitor Facebook frequently so you can stop a problem before it goes viral.

Another question we frequently hear is from roofing contractors with multiple locations. "How do the search engines determine the reputation of our company if we're in several towns?" Here's the reality if you have multiple offices. While it's the same company, it is multiple locations to the search engines and the prospects looking for a roofing contractor in each city. That means you need to do all of the work of claiming your listing on the review sites and building your places page for each of the search engines for every location. If you have offices in three cities you'll need three places pages and to claim the top dozen or sites at a minimum for each location.

One more question has to do with the weather. For those contractors who can only roof six to eight months a year, but run another business in the winter, how do you handle reputation marketing? If your winter business uses a different name and is a completely different business from your roofing company, then you'll need to do all the steps I've described for that business as well. If you do roofing in the summer but remodel kitchens in the winter, and use the same business name for both activities, you only need to claim your sites one time.

Keep in mind that most of the review sites use your primary business telephone number as their method of identifying your company. So if you do run both businesses using the same main number you'll want to talk about the two companies in the description section of the listings you claim.

Whether you follow some of the steps I've outlined in this chapter and on the webinar, or use another system for getting and marketing positive reviews for your company, Reputation Marketing is vital to your ability to gain market share and increase profitability. Start today!

WHAT TO DO NOW:

1. If you haven't already done so, go to www.business.google.com and claim your free Google My Business listing.

2. Claim the primary citation sites for your business. For a roofing company you want to be listed on the following: Google My Business, Yelp, Foursquare, Insiderpages, Citysearch, and Superpages. Keep in mind that most of these sites have an option to pay monthly for an "upgraded" listing. This is not necessary, just use the free services.

Finding and claiming your business on these sites can be a little confusing. I suggest that you Google the instructions for each one. For example, "how do I register my business on foursquare."

Then just follow the directions.

3. You also want to claim your "places" listing on Bing and Yahoo. These require more information to be fully optimized. Again, do a Google search on how to claim and complete your listings.

4. Decide how you are going to invite past customers to review your business. At the very least you'll want to contact all customers from the past year. A business card or postcard with instructions and a link to where you'd like them to leave their review works well. Just realize that you'll have to send these four or five times over a couple of months to get a good response. A phone call at about the time the postcard arrives will increase response rates.

5. Where are you going to have your customers post their reviews? If you have an agency working for you that uses one of the third party programs I mentioned, then talk with them about the priority location you want people to leave reviews on. Generally, this will be your Google page.

6. Every time you have a meeting with your employees, both office and field workers, include a conversation about customer service and the importance of creating a 5 star reputation on line. Read reviews that have been posted to your team. Anytime someone on your team is mentioned in a positive comment from a customer make sure that is posted for all to see. Some of our clients even offer a cash bonus (nothing big, $20) when a customer singles them out for providing excellent service. The point is to make everyone aware of the role they play in this important focus.

* * * * * * * * * * *

This has been a long chapter, but is possibly the most important information I can share with you to help your business grow. The online reputation of your company is critical to your success. I encourage you to implement these steps as soon as you can.

Gordon Van Wechel

Your Website: How You Establish Trust With A Prospect

Would it surprise you to learn that more than 40% of the small business owners in America today do not see the value in having a website for their business? That's according to Entrepreneur Magazine, who researched the question in a national survey. In a similar study Yodle, the online marketing firm, calculated 44% of businesses do not have a website.

Which begs the obvious question: do you? If the answer is yes then here is my follow up question: is your website bringing new prospects to your roofing business? Do you know? How can you turn your website into a leads machine?

In this chapter I'm going to talk about websites, and do so in a way that you may not be expecting. I don't believe that your website should just be an "electronic billboard" for your business. In many cases the first contact a prospect has with your company is your website. The Home Page of your sight is where they decide if you offer anything of value to them, and is it worth it to continue to look on your site to learn more about your firm.

Here is an interesting fact. According to Google, the average time that a person spends on a website is between 10 and 12 seconds! What that statistic means is that in most cases a prospect glances at your home page, doesn't find an immediate answer to the questions in their mind or something of interest that compels them to read more, and they move on to a competitor's site. You have lost the opportunity to engage with them...all in just a few seconds!

Let me share some website strategies that will help you connect with a prospect, capture their attention and engage their interest so that you have a better chance they will take the next step with you.

In the process of doing this, I'm also going to share two foundational marketing concepts that you may not be familiar with: the Educational Spectrum and the Marketing Equation. But first, let's talk about "trust."

Creating Trust With A Prospect

My belief is that the primary purpose of your website is to build in the mind of your prospect the belief that you and your company can be trusted. What does that mean? Several things:

- You will help them understand the process of getting a new roof. You'll answer questions they don't yet know to ask.
- If it is an insurance job, you will assist in dealing with the adjustors and all the paperwork associated with their claim.
- Your company can offer the proper materials for their home, and explain why you are suggesting the products you are.
- The people who come to install the roof will do a professional job and not cause damage to their home.
- If there is an issue at anytime during the process, you will take care of it.
- Your company will be around in the future. You stand behind your work.

How do you convey these concepts on a website? Here are

several suggestions.

1. Put your <u>local</u> telephone number in a prominent place on the top right hand side of your home page. It should be in a larger font size, and very easy to find. There have been numerous studies of how a person's eyes scan the home page of a website. Immediately when the page opens they start at the top left, and quickly scan across the menu bar. Their eyes naturally stop at the top right corner, and then begin to move down the page, typically in a "Z" pattern. By putting your telephone number in that upper right portion of the screen, the viewer's eye will naturally stop there. Even if they don't call at that moment, subconsciously they have registered that your number is in that location for future reference.

2. In the area "above the fold" it is critical that you speak directly to the conversation in the mind of your prospect. (Above the fold is an old newspaper term that refers to the top half of the front page of the paper. On your website it is the area on the screen before someone begins to scroll down.)

There are several ways to use this area effectively. A popular trend today is with a Gallery. This is a series for four or five images that automatically scroll every two or three seconds. This gives you an opportunity to feature some of your previous jobs as well as your company. The viewers natural curiosity is triggered by the moving photos, they want to stay around and see what is next.

If you use a gallery don't just show the biggest homes you've ever worked on. Someone who owns an average size home will think you're an expensive company that only focuses on the higher end homes. Consider an image of one of your crews, on the jobsite or a portrait style photo in front of your offices. If you have specialties, metal roofs for example, be sure to include one of these jobs.

It can be effective to add a few words of text over the image. Use phrases that are important to the prospect, not just platitudes that say how great your company is. Remember, your primary goal is to engender trust in the mind of the prospect.

3. If you offer any type of financing, or have contracted with one of the financing companies that offer programs for home improvement, feature their clickable banner at the top of the page. I realize that this can look a little cheesy, advertising another company on your website. However, for any prospect that is not dealing with an insurance claim, this could be the difference between your company getting the job and one of your competitors winning the business.

We have put these banners on several contractor websites, and in every case seen the requests for an estimate and telephone inquiries increase by at least 15%! If you offer this service, let people know quickly.

4. If the Home page is the most important on your website, the "About Us" page is a close second. This is where you tell the story of your company. It is important to include the facts; how long you've been in business, the product lines you represent, etc. Even more important is a personal profile of you, the owner. Include photos, not just you but also key people on your team.

5. Video is a powerful way to generate that trust you are looking for on your website. In fact, consumer surveys indicate that more than 70% of people "trust" a company that has a video on their website more than a competitor who does not.

Where to use video? Instead of the Gallery I mentioned earlier, have a video featuring the owner briefly describing how your company works with home and business owners to resolve roofing problems. Identify two or at the most three of the "value propositions" that you offer. This video should be no more than two minutes in length, and you should be looking directly into the camera as you speak to the prospects visiting your site.

If you have the proverbial "great face for radio" to paraphrase an old joke, or are just not comfortable in front of the camera, consider using one of your managers. Or have an animated video created that introduces your company. We often see what are called "white board" videos used effectively to accomplish this.

Another place where video is effective is on the About Us page. Here you should only feature the owner and focus on telling the story of the company. Remember, this is the second most important page on your site.

6. Include a Frequently Asked Questions page. This is a great place to establish your credibility as an expert. Even more than that, here is where you can anticipate and answer sales objections in advance.

7. Include a "Reviews" page on your menu bar, not "Testimonials." The emphasis on reviews and a business's Star Rating has become so prominent in the last three years that prospects are naturally attuned to looking for your reviews. I talk about this more in the Reputation chapter. Consider using one of the review capture programs that can be added as a page to your website displaying your reviews.

8. The Contact Us page for most websites is just a form that asks a prospect for their personal information and guarantees that a

salesperson will be contacting them. For that reason most visitors to your site will not complete the form.

To improve the response rate, add a couple of paragraphs at the top of this form that thank the prospect for contacting you, and then describe what will happen after someone fills out the form. Share your process with them and more people will be comfortable letting you contact them.

This is another place where a short video can be a powerful tool.

Generating Leads With Your Website

If you have done a good job of creating trust with your website, you will want to capitalize on that by offering the visitor an easy way to take the next step with your company. Most roofing company sites do that with a Contact Us box on at least one of the pages offering a "free estimate." This essentially tells the prospect, "give us your information so one of our sales people can call you."

But what about the person who isn't ready to talk with a sales person yet? Maybe they're just starting to consider a new roof, and don't even know what questions to ask at this point. If the only option with your company is to invite a sales person over to their home, you have probably just lost them.

Instead, consider one or more information filled reports on subjects that are relevant to them that can be easily downloaded from your website. To access a report the prospect will give you their email address, but not a phone number. This is a much easier, 'baby step' in their process of educating themselves about buying a new roof.

The reports can be short, just a couple of pages of good information that is responding to a specific question many prospects ask. It should be focused on the prospect, and not an advertisement for your company. At the end of the report you can certainly add a paragraph or two about you and your company, but do not make the report one of those "advertorials" that you see in newspapers so often these days.

Make sure your report is written to answer the prospects questions. A report on the differences between GAF shingles and Owens-Corning shingles is not relevant to someone considering a new roof. To the consumer a shingle is a shingle and whatever subtleties you see between the brands is lost on the homeowner.

Why is this strategy so important (and effective)? Let me introduce you to the concept of the Educational Spectrum and I think it will be clear.

The Educational Spectrum

At the beginning of this chapter I promised to introduce you to two marketing concepts you might not be familiar with. These are foundational for under-standing how to make your advertising more effective and increase your market share. The first of these is the Educational Spectrum.

Think back over the last year or so to the customers who you have worked with. With the exception of someone who has sustained roof damage from a weather event and has an immediate need for a new roof, how did your customers come to you? Through one of your marketing channels or as a referral from another past customer are the two most likely scenarios.

Now as you think about those customers, did very many of them wake up one morning, say to themselves, "I think I'll buy a new roof today?" Not likely. In fact, most of them spent some time looking on the Internet for advice, may have shopped at one of the big box home improvement stores to get some information, and probably asked their neighbors for a recommendation.

In other words, they invested some time educating themselves before making a commitment to a major investment like a new roof. We call that process the "Educational Spectrum" and all prospects follow this pattern when considering a large investment like a new roof.

To better understand this concept, visualize a line with numbers from one through ten along its length. This line represents all of the people who live in the city or market area where you offer roofing services.

1   5   10

The people at the far left, numbers one and two, will never need your service at any time and are not prospects. They rent their home or live in an apartment and will never be candidates for your offer. At the other end, the 10's, are your past customers who think you have the best roofing company ever. They are tremendously pleased with the job you did for them, refer others to you, and have become 'raving fans' of your company. Everyone in between, the 3's through 9's, are prospective customers.

As a prospect moves towards the right side of this continuum, they are closer to actually pulling out their checkbook and signing a contract for their new roof. Now think about it. When someone is over at an 8 or 9 what is their primary motivation? If you said price you are correct. By the time a prospect gets to that side of the Education Spectrum they are already committed to replacing their roof, have a good idea about the materials, and are really just price shopping. Sales managers call these prospects who are ready to buy the "low hanging fruit" and encourage salespeople to look for them.

Why? Why do you want to spend your time talking with shoppers who are focused on getting the lowest price? Even if you have a great 'Inside Reality' and offer a much better product and service, the 'Outside Perception' of this buyer is that price is the primary point of differentiation. (If you've forgotten these terms, please go back to the Foundations chapter where I introduce the concept of Inside Reality and Outside Perception.)

What if you could begin a conversation with the prospect back when they are a three, four, or five, as they are beginning to do their research about putting a new roof on their home? What if you had the opportunity to share with them the great 'Inside Reality' of your company, the value proposition that sets you apart from your competition and makes you worth their business, even if your price is higher?

That's the value of establishing trust through your website. Most people who begin to research a topic will go to the Internet. They'll type into their browser something like, "roof replacement Sacramento" or "roofing contractor Miami" and begin to scan through the first two pages. (Statistically, according to Google, less than 10% of internet searches go past page two.)

They may see a Pay Per Click ad and select it. If you are fortunate, your organic website listing is on those first two pages. You may have one or more properly optimized videos that show on these pages and take the shopper to your site through a link. Maybe you're listed in the Maps section and they can link to you that way. Whatever the path, they identify several companies and click through to their company websites.

Now is when the real value of creating a trust focused lead generation website becomes obvious. Remember my point a couple of pages ago about how everyone's brochure site looks the same? How that leads a prospect to conclude that all companies are essentially the same so price becomes their only concern?

If you have a Lead Gen website it will immediately jump out as different, for several reasons. First, a headline that is relevant to someone thinking about replacing their roof. Instead of the "we're the best" platitudes that your competitors offer, you join the conversation that is in the mind of the prospect by offering valuable information that answers their questions. You do that by offering to send them a report that will further elaborate on what they want/need to know about buying a new roof.

In addition to the report, you may have other offers that give the prospect the opportunity to move to the next step in the Educational Spectrum in a way that is comfortable for them. Instead of "call for a free estimate" like everyone else, you might offer a recorded message detailing the "Seven Questions to Ask A Roofing Contractor Before Hiring Them." As they jump around on your website there are other offers, for example a report on "Working With Your Insurance Adjuster to Minimize Your Out of Pocket Expense on a New Roof."

What the prospect experiences when coming to your Lead Gen site is a wealth of information, answers to their questions, and the questions they didn't know to ask. They will see the typical testimonials from past customers, photos of completed jobs, and a way to contact you. What they won't experience is every page asking them to call for an appointment. The prospect can move along at their own pace.

The result is that when they are ready to call several contractors to come over and give an estimate, your company is included in that group.

A Lead Generation website requires a different thought process for a business owner. Most of us seem to have learned about marketing by looking at the Yellow Pages. At least that's what I think when I look at a lot of roofing company websites. At the top is the company name, maybe a slogan (but really a platitude). Then there is a list of services kind of like a menu board at the local deli. At the end is a call to action, something like "call for a free estimate" and a phone number in bold type.

Really? Think about it. When you see an advertisement like that do you ever stop and read it? I mean actually read all the copy and think to yourself, "hmmm, maybe I should call them." Almost never! Why? Because the ad doesn't say anything about what the potential customer is interested in--their 'hot buttons.' *The ad is all about the company and nothing about the prospect.*

When I work with a client to help them enhance their marketing there are several exercises I ask them to complete. While a detailed explanation of each of these is beyond the scope of this chapter, let me give you a quick overview designed to help make you a better advertising copy writer.

Effective copy speaks to the needs of the potential customer--it is focused on the conversation in their mind about your product or service. You prospect doesn't care if you've been in business since 1876 and have the greatest group of employees since George Washington picked his first Cabinet. All a prospect cares about is having their personal needs met. If you can demonstrate your ability to do that in your advertising, then you have a chance to capture their attention and eventually their business.

So how do you do that?

A good place to begin is with the Customer Discovery Questions I suggested in the Foundations chapter. This exercise is based on the belief that "If you want to know what John Smith buys, you have to see the world through John Smith's eyes." That is, until you understand what is important to your customer, you can't write effective advertising copy.

Many times when we begin this exercise, it is the first time our client has actually stopped and thought about what might be important to their customer. It can be a very revealing experience! Most of us as business owners are so focused on what we offer that we rarely stop and think about how a prospective client views or experiences our company and our team. It can be sobering to realize how much money we have left on the table over the time we've been in business because of this ignorance.

I encourage you to spend some quiet time thinking about these questions and write down your thoughts. Ask your key employees to do the same and compare your answers. It can be a very revealing experience!

The Marketing Equation

Since writing copy for a Lead Gen website, and your other marketing, is going to require a new way of thinking, I want to share with you what we call The Marketing Equation. This idea is based on the belief that marketing is science, not art. That by understanding more about our customer, seeing the world through their eyes, we can craft our advertising statements to speak to the conversation in their mind and win the right to talk further with them.

The Marketing Equation has four components. As I describe them, I want you to think about an advertisement you will be writing for your business. It could be a flyer, newspaper ad, the homepage of your website, or the ad you are going to put on a postcard. Here are the components:

1. Interrupt--getting qualified prospects to pay attention to your marketing. Think of this as the headline for your ad. It must be based on the hot buttons that are important to your prospect. It should answer one or more of the Discovery Questions you thought through earlier. Here are some hints:

- Your company name is not a hot button headline for your prospect. DO NOT put it at the top of your advertisements.
- No "False Betas." A false beta is an interrupt that has no relevance to your company or product. For example, putting a woman in a bikini in your roofing company ad. While you will catch the eye of many people looking at your ad, once they realize the image has no congruence with your product or service they will move on and never read the rest of your ad.
- A question can be a good interrupt, but it is difficult to phrase in broad enough terms to interrupt a large cross section of the readership. It is better to make a declarative statement.

2. Engage--think of this as a sub-headline. What you are saying to your reader is that "if you continue to read, there is information coming that will help in your decision making process about my product or service."

3. Educate--identify important issues for the prospect and demonstrate how you solve them. For most marketing campaigns bullet points are a great way to do this. On your website you can use more copy, but keep it focused on the customer.

4. Offer--give them a low risk way to take the next step in the buying process. You want to make your prospect feel like they're in charge. The next step may be coming into your place of business, but it could also be requesting a report or visiting a web page. Too often we try to jump from first meeting a prospect to handing them a contract and asking for their signature. Just like when you were dating, the sales process requires a time of wooing. This is particularly true in a highly competitive marketplace like the roofing industry.

Let me give just one example of how this works in a "real world" setting--writing an advertisement to go on a postcard. I'll make this really generic so you can visualize a variety of companies using the format.

1. Interrupt: On the front side of the card I'd have a full color image, maybe a member of an install crew on the roof. Over the top of the photo is this Interrupt (headline):

3 Critical Characteristics to Demand From Your Roofing Contractor

2. The "Engage" portion, or sub headline. How about something like:

Do You Know What They Are?

OK, with just those few words you have the attention of anyone who has been thinking about needing a new roof. We still haven't told them the name of our company, or any of the great slogans we've come up with that describe how wonderful we are. But you know what? Right now they are turning over the postcard to learn more...and that's the whole point! Let's keep going.

3. Educate. What are those 3 Critical Characteristics? Here is where we tell them. And because we only have part of a postcard to do so, bullet points are the logical way to do it. What do we put in the bullet points? We speak directly to the issues in the mind of the prospect we identified in the Discovery Questions exercise. For example

- Expertise. (Make a few word statement about the level of experience and excellence a prospect should expect. Obviously you can meet this criteria).
- Value. (Here is where you briefly address their concern about cost of the service or product).
- Customer Experience. (What you do to make the customer feel comfortable shopping with you.

4. Offer. Now you put your company name and tell them the specific next step you want them to take.

XYZ Roofers. Go to www.xyzreport.com to get your free report and see how We Stack Up.

OK, obviously those exact terms won't work for all situations. The point was to give you an example of an ad that follows the Marketing Equation, an ad that actually addresses the needs of your prospects. When you stop and think about it, it is easier to structure an ad like this than to try and cram in a lot of generalities and platitudes that really don't tell your prospect anything.

That was a postcard, how does it apply to a website? Follow the same formula. The only exception I make is when designing a home page I do put the company name near the top of the page. It is in smaller type than what you usually see, and is secondary to the headline and offer that always appear near the top of the screen. Other than that the steps are exactly the same.

If we are creating a site using the Gallery of Images for the home page that I mentioned earlier, I'll put a few words of text over each image that speaks to a specific need or question a prospect is asking. These become the "Interrupt."

The Marketing Equation applies to your PPC ads, landing pages, flyers, door hangers; every advertising piece you might create should follow this formula!

To summarize, your website must be focused on the customer and their needs, not the company. It is not an 'electronic brochure' that offers a list of features that you believe are important, without sharing the benefit to your customer of each of those features. It always offers an easy way for the prospect to take the next step along the Education Spectrum at a pace that is comfortable for them. That is typically in the form of a free report offering information that is valuable to the prospect.

Of course your site will include secondary pages for testimonials, job photos, information about your company and team members; the traditional pages that people who dig deeply into your site expect. The difference is that these too are written to help the customer get to know your Inside Reality in a way that is meaningful to them.

WHAT TO DO NOW

1. If you want an effective Lead Gen site you are going to have to be more proactive with the graphics person and site designer you work with than is normal. Most designers are used to creating "brochure" sites and don't understand the why and how of building a site that is truly a marketing tool and not just "pretty."

I suggest you make a detailed sketch of how you want your home page to look, and the overall appearance of the rest of the pages. If you are creating a Word Press site, work with your designer to find a theme that easily facilitates this. (My preference is a three column theme as it offers a lot of flexibility for individual page construction.)

2. What is going to be the offer on your home page? I suggest a free report with a title that speaks directly to the interests of the prospective customer. Here are some examples of reports we've done:

"6 Things Your Insurance Company Won't Tell You About Getting A New Roof"

"10 Easy Things You Can Do To Add Years To The Life Of Your Roof"

"7 Questions to Ask A Roofing Contractor Before Letting Them on Your Roof"

Can you see how each of these speaks to the conversation in the mind of someone considering the purchase of a new roof? Obviously the report should help the prospect understand how your company meets all of the criteria established in the report. It is not a blatant "commercial" for your company, but should put questions in the mind of the prospect that you can answer positively as they come to you after reading.

Write the report(s) and identify what is needed for any other offers you might make on the site.

3. One of the reasons you offer the free report is to capture the prospects email address. This allows you to send them interesting and valuable information over a short period of time via email. This further solidifies you as an expert who is focused on offering value, not just asking for an appointment.

The tool you'll need to do this is called an auto-responder. It is a software program that allows you to create a series of emails that are delivered on a preprogrammed schedule you determine. Your auto-responder system will also "host" your free report and deliver automatically when someone fills out the form on your website.

There are at least a dozen auto-responder companies you can choose from. I have used several of them and find an auto-responder to be a valuable tool for your business marketing. Here are three that are easy to learn and have a low monthly cost:

www.aweber.com   This may be the most popular in the marketplace.

www.getresponse.com This is the program that we currently use at Alchemy.

www.mailchimp.com This is the least expensive system I'm aware of.

Choose an auto-responder program for your company. Write a

series of six to eight short, information packed emails that can be delivered over a period of fourteen to twenty days after a prospect orders your report. Also upload your report to the auto-responder and create the form code your web designer will need to put the opt-in form on your site.

Most web designers will have experience with these steps and can help you complete them. Of course you'll want to write the report and email copy yourself.

4. Continue to market your website in all of your other marketing pieces. If you have not yet started a Reputation Marketing program for your company, consider doing so quickly as this will help your site's organic positioning with the search engines.

Gordon Van Wechel

Getting Found Online--Getting to the First Two Pages is Discipline Over Time, Not A Magic Formula

The "good old days" of building a website and having your prospects find it easily are long gone. The struggle to get found online in today's Internet is perhaps the biggest marketing challenge faced by roofing contractors.

Here's the reality. There are just ten listings on the first page of Google available for all of the companies in your market area. In most cities when I search keywords related to the roofing industry, I see at least four of these taken up by the national brands: Home Advisor, Angie's List, the Better Business Bureau, Yelp, and at least one of those "10 Best" list sites. That leaves somewhere between four and six potential listings for local companies.

There is also the "map pack" or "3 pack" of companies that are highlighted in the space just below the paid ads and above the organic listings. This is the most coveted position on the page as in many markets 60% of the prospects looking for your services click on companies in this area. In some cities we're starting to see Google "sell" one of these listings, reserving it for a paid ad.

You Can't Fool Mother Google

Do you want to take a guess on how many times each year Google makes a change in the algorithm that determines which websites are presented on page one of the search results? In 2017 there were more than 300 changes *that they told us about*. That's more than one every business day of the year!

These are not major changes that you read about in the news, the Hummingbird or Penguin Updates. They are just little tweaks designed to make sure that the best possible results are offered to the searcher for the keywords they search.

Given those two facts, the intense competition for a first page listing and the frequency with which Google moves the target, it seems nearly impossible for a company to climb to the first page for any valuable keyword. That is not exactly true.

While it is difficult to achieve a top listing, and takes a dedicated effort over time, Google also is transparent, telling us what they are prioritizing with their algorithm as they make these changes. Right now, in the middle of 2018, there are three primary activities you can focus on to enhance your position in the search results. These are:

- Your companies online reputation, as defined by your "Star Rating"
- High quality backlinks to your website
- The click through rate and dwell time metrics for your site

In this chapter I'll go into more detail on each of these. First let me describe some basic SEO activities that every business needs.

Foundations for Getting Found Online

1. Google My Business (GMB) page. Every company has a free listing on Google, but you have to claim and optimize it to have a benefit. Think of your GMB page as an enhanced Yellow Pages listing. On it you confirm the location of your business, operating hours, payment terms and other basic information. You can also upload photos relevant to your business, and even video content.

I like to describe your Google My Business listing as the cornerstone of your presence on the internet. Other citation and directory sites look first to your GMB page to verify information about your business. Plus, it is a repository for your customer reviews on Google, and a place where someone can leave a review.

If you're not sure if you've claimed your GMB page, start by entering this link into a browser window: business.google.com. On the upper right of the page that opens up you'll see a green box that says "Start Now." Click that and follow the directions. In most cases, once you've entered your business information Google will send a verification postcard to your address. This postcard will have a numeric code on it that you'll have to go back into your listing and enter to finish the process.

This is a mandatory first step to helping your website appear in the search results more frequently, and to begin the climb to page one.

2. Citation/Directory Sites. These are online information sites that collect information on businesses. Many of them also allow visitors to leave a review about a business. Some of the better know citation sites are Yelp, Yellow Book, Trip Advisor, and Hot Frog.

At last count there are more than 2000 of these citation and directory sites. Many are specific to a business niche, for example: dentists. How many do you need to claim for your roofing business? The answer to this question changes over time, but right now we are claiming 30 to 50 sites for our clients. I say "right now" because not too long ago we'd routinely register 250 or more for each client. What Google is now telling us is that they are more interested in the quality of link created by registering with a site than the number of sites. We now focus on claiming those sites that are relevant to both the city our client operates in and the roofing niche, but that also have a page authority rating of at least 25.

We also analyze your competition--what sites have they claimed--and make certain we include as many of those as meet the criteria I just mentioned in your campaign.

The process for claiming these sites can be arduous. Once you identify the sites you want it is necessary to log into each of them individually and follow the steps they give for registering. Some will just accept your submission, others will want to verify the data. The rule to follow here is to make certain that what you enter is exactly the same as your Google My Business listing. When I say "exactly" I'm serious. If your GMB shows your address as "123 Main Street, Ste. 2" then for every site you claim you need to enter "123 Main Street, Ste. 2". Even if your normally spell out Suite, it is important that all citation and directory sites are the same as your GMB listing.

There are many services you can find online that will do this for you. Most offer what seems like a great deal, "350 sites for $80" as an example. On the surface that is a good value, but then you get your report of the work they've done and realize that the 350 sites they've claimed are almost all irrelevant to your business and city. What good is claiming the Detroit Yellow Book listing when your business is in Little Rock?

Most of these services have identified sites they can claim using software with very little human interaction, which is why they are so cheap. They are also claiming sites with very low page authority, which defeats the purpose of the whole exercise.

Another service to be wary of is Yext. While they do a great job of claiming mostly relevant sites for you, their program requires a monthly financial commitment to "maintain" the sites. If you ever get tired of paying this, they disconnect the links they have created and you are back to starting over. Monthly monitoring of the sites you've claimed is not necessary. At the most, two times a year you should go to the site and verify that the information is still correct.

Something else to consider is the four "aggregator sites." Think about the credit reporting agencies, there are three major ones that the credit card and mortgage companies use to track your credit. In the same way, there are four aggregator sites that the other citation and directory sites link with and use to update their own records. The four sites are Axciom, Factual, Infogroup, and Neustar. Claiming your business on these sites is a little more time consuming, and it can take them several months to acknowledge your submission, but over time they can be a benefit for keeping your online information consistently accurate.

Local Search Optimization

The search engines make it a priority to try and localize search results to a close proximity relative to the searchers location. The goal is to try and provide vendors within a three mile radius. If there are not enough results, then they expand to five miles, etc.

This can be an added challenge for contractors working in large metropolitan areas. Let's say your office address is on the west side of Denver, in the community known as Lakewood. If a homeowner in Aurora, a suburb on the far east of Denver, searches for a roofing contractor there is almost no chance that your company will be included in the search results. Why? Because there are many other contractors who are closer to the address of the searcher.

One way you can broaden your opportunities is by listing all of the communities you serve in the footer section of your website. This may seem cumbersome since most prospects don't scroll down that far on your page, but the search engine spiders crawl the footer and register all of these community "keywords."

A powerful strategy we implement for our clients is to create what we call "city pages." These are full pages of content, a minimum of 750 words, that refer to your services in a specific suburb. We highlight two or three of the clients primary keywords within this content, always referencing them within the context of the "city" that is featured on that page.

Take the example I just mentioned of the Lakewood contractor who is not appearing in an Aurora search. If you create a page of content that focuses on several of your services in Aurora and then publish it as part of your website, the search engine spiders will crawl that page and begin to connect your company with roofing services in Aurora. Repeat this for every suburban area around Denver (there are more than a dozen of them) and you have started a "City Pages" strategy. Do this every quarter, highlighting two or three different keywords each quarter, and you will increase the opportunity to be presented in search results throughout your market area.

You can make these pages even more powerful by creating "internal links" that take the search engine spiders to several other pages of your site while they are there. Internal links are evidence to the spiders that yours is a well thought out and designed site.

Another bonus is that every quarter you are uploading fresh

content to the site. Google likes to see active websites that are consistently adding new information that will be valuable to the searcher. When you upload your city pages and ask the search engines to re-index your site they give you credit for providing this fresh content.

When I describe this strategy to people they immediately respond that they don't want to mess up their website with a lot of extra pages that will just confuse people. I agree. The answer is to upload these pages into your website *but not make them visible to visitors*. In the dashboard of your website you can specify how a page is treated, and in this case mark them as not public. The search engine spiders crawl all of the pages on your website, not just those that are "public" and listed in the menu on your home page.

Optimizing your website for local search is the first important step in more frequent presentation in the search results.

The 3 Primary Algorithm Components (Today)

I mentioned earlier that there are three significant parts of Google's algorithm that determine which websites are presented to searchers. Now let me define them and share how to best take advantage.

1. Your online reputation. I write extensively about this in the chapter on reputation, so let me refer you to that chapter if you haven't read it yet.

2. Backlinks from high page authority websites.

"Backlink" is one of those terms that we in the online advertising business throw around like everyone should know what it means.

I don't want to make that assumption, so let's start with a definition and what it really means in practical terms for your business.

When a webpage links to any other page it's called a backlink. Every page on your website has its own distinct URL address. Backlinks can come to any page, not just your home page. In years past backlinks were the primary indicator to Google that a site had relevance for specific keywords. That is no longer the case, but backlinks are still an important part of the algorithm.

There are several ways to get backlinks for your website. The most effective is to write good quality articles and blog posts and publish them. If you have a blog on your site that is the first place to publish, but you can also used LinkedIn and other social media sites. There are quite a few roofing industry related groups on LinkedIn that you can publish your article on.

A second method is to make comments on publications by other group members or in industry related forums. In the signature line of your post you can list your website URL, creating a back link. If you do this make good comments that demonstrate that you have actually read the article. Spam comments stand out very quickly and can result in you being banned from the group.

Another way to generate backlinks is to submit your blog post or article to web directories. This can be a little dicey as some directories have been created for the sole purpose of generating backlinks. These generally do not last for very long as the search engines will block them. If you are considering a directory as a place to post make sure you do not join one that asks you to create a back link to their website as a requirement for joining.

As you develop a plan to generate backlinks for your website you will soon run into one of the many automated direct submission services. DO NOT succumb to the temptation to use these! They will spread your article across many sites, most with very low domain authority, and make it appear to be spam. This will cost you in domain authority for your own site, and potentially cause your blog to be completely removed from the search engines.

If a search engine optimization company promises to get you quality backlinks at what seems to be a bargain price it is because they are using article spinning and automated submission software. Here again you run the risk of incurring penalties for spam.

There is no shortcut to creating quality content and publishing it appropriately. It takes time, but the value of the backlinks created will help your website move up in the search results. If you can't do this yourself, make sure you ask the right questions of any agency you consider engaging. If they take shortcuts it is you who will suffer the penalty.

3. Click Through Rate and Dwell Time

This component in the search engine algorithm is simple arithmetic. Click through rate is calculated by dividing the number of times your website is presented in the search results by the number of searchers who select your site. The challenge here is that it doesn't matter whether your site is listed on page one or page five. The more that people click on your site, the more frequently it will be presented...with one caveat: dwell time.

Dwell time is how long someone spends on your website once they select it, and is the more important metric. Any guess about the average time someone stays on a website these day? According to Google it is between ten and twelve seconds! That means that a high percentage of the time people click on a site, don't immediately see something they want, and then hit the back button and look for another site.

A short dwell time says to the search engine that your website did not provide the searcher with valuable information for the keyword they searched, so your site should not be presented as frequently in the search results for that keyword. We have seen contractors try to influence this by having their staff members log onto the company website and stay for several minutes. This does not help as the search engines recognize the IP address of your network and count all of these visits as one and not several.

The best way to impact dwell time is to have compelling content on your homepage, something that arrests the searchers attention long enough for them to begin to interact with your page and then move on to additional pages. A good strategy is a short video that welcomes the visitor and tells them what they will learn by visiting your site. Another currently popular technique is to create a gallery of three to five images that scroll across the page, with a two or three second interval between images.

At Alchemy we've developed relationships with a network of individuals, primarily senior citizens, who work a few hours a week doing searches. We provide them with the keywords to search and our clients business name. They search for the company in the search results and click on it (click through rate), going as far as page ten to find the correct website. Then they spend a minimum of one minute on the site and review no fewer than two pages (dwell time).

There are other agencies with similar methods. If you decide to outsource the work to get your website found more easily then ask about this.

Paid Advertising

For many newer companies, or even established businesses who are in highly competitive markets, moving to the first two pages for the most important keywords is time consuming and difficult. The answer here is to "buy" a position by using Google Adwords. I write in another chapter about Pay Per Click advertising and I encourage you to review that information as you consider strategies to get discovered on line.

I began this chapter by pointing out the difficulty in having your website presented on the first page of search results. Difficult, yes. Impossible, no. Getting Found Online is a process that requires consistent work across several strategies. If you can maintain this effort over time you will see results.

WHAT TO DO NOW:

1. If you have not claimed your Google My Business page then get this done as soon as possible. Once your site is verified, begin to work on claiming citation and directory sites. You want at least 25 of these.

2. Getting found online is not something you work on occasionally, it requires a well designed plan and consistent activity over time to be successful. I have briefly described some of the strategies we find to be the most effective at this time. This is not a complete list, there are other activities that will lead to better presentation of your company in the search results, but those I've shared will give the best potential for quickly advancing.

If you have a marketing person on your staff then work with them to develop a written GFO plan. Be sure to define how you are going to measure success so you can monitor a return on your investment.

The alternative is hiring an outside agency for this important activity. Here again make sure you identify specific actions they will be taking, and how you'll measure success.

Video Marketing--Putting the World's #2 Search Engine To Work For You

Not too many years ago, if you thought about "video marketing" your only option was to produce and broadcast television commercials. While expensive, for many roofing companies it was the best way to get prospects calling. As local cable advertising rates and video production costs have dropped, this can still be a powerful business growth strategy for you company.

Here's some good news: you don't have to hire an ad agency and expensive camera crews to produce top quality marketing videos any more. In fact, with a smart phone and just a little creativity you can create dynamic marketing pieces that will inform, teach, engage, and amuse people. Nor do you need to buy a package of air time from your local cable provider. Now you can "broadcast" your videos on YouTube, Vimeo, Daily Motion, Hulu, and at least a dozen more video websites.

In this chapter I want to demonstrate the importance and simplicity of video marketing for your business. Here's how I'm going to do that:

- Some startling facts showing why you need video marketing
- Types of videos to shoot
- How to get started producing quality videos for your business
- How to Set up a YouTube channel
- Strategies for marketing your videos

Why You Need Video Marketing

If you have any doubts about video as a marketing tool for your company, here are some facts compiled in early 2017, along with the sources of the data:

- YouTube has 1 billion unique visitors each month. (Huff Post)
- Just under 5 billion videos are watched on YouTube each day (Videoniche)
- 52% of consumers say that watching a video makes them more confident in online purchases (Inovodo)
- 55% of marketers who use video in their email campaigns reported an increase in click through rate (eMarketer)
- 9% of US Small businesses use YouTube (FortuneLords)
- 82% of marketers plan to add video to their sites, making it a higher priority than Facebook, Twitter, and blog integration (Social Media Examiner)
- Videos on landing pages increased conversions by 86% (WebDAM)

So the question is no longer, "do I need any videos to market my roofing business?" The question should be, "how can I incorporate video into my company marketing quickly and easily?"

Video? What Do I Do That Should Be On A Video?

You may be surprised to learn that most of what you do in your business is worth shooting a short video about. Remember that when people are searching for a roofing contractor they don't know what to ask. They've heard horror stories about the storm chasers who do sloppy work and then disappear. All they want to do is find someone they feel they can trust to do a good job at a fair price. The purpose of your video marketing is to let them get to know you, your team, and the quality of work you do.

Video is far more compelling than anything written you can put on your website to facilitate this "know-like-trust" process.

Here are some ideas for types of videos you might consider:

1. Testimonials. Perhaps the most powerful marketing you can do is a short video with a homeowner right after finishing their job. These are quite simple to shoot, and require almost no preparation. Here are some tips:

- An ideal length is 30 to 45 seconds. This gives you enough time to ask no more than two questions and let the homeowner respond.
- You'll be shooting using the natural light available that day. Make sure not to shoot in such a way that the sun is behind the people or their faces will be obscured.
- Location should be in the yard with the house and new roof readily visible in the background. I like the front yard, as it is usually less cluttered.
- Position your yard sign so that it is visible, but down in the lower right corner as you compose the shot.
- Two ways to do these videos, and creating a library that is a mixture of both is best. One is to have the crew manager standing with the people, look to the camera and introduce them, ask one or two questions, say thank you, and it's done. It is a very quick conversation where they are looking at each other, not into the camera once the introduction is made. For this video format another crew member will shoot the video.

- The second method is to have the homeowner(s) only in the shot, let them introduce themselves, and then mention two things they especially appreciated about your company, the crew, and the job. You will prompt them with the subjects before they start, but there is not someone asking them questions, it is their "candid" impressions. In this case they will be looking into the camera.

The questions and subjects we want people to address are the "hot buttons" that are in the minds of prospective customers who will be watching these. For example:

- How your company took care of dealing with the insurance company
- Protecting plants, windows, patio, etc when doing the work
- Getting good value for the money spent, a quality job with quality materials
- Are the crews professional looking and talking, or are they derelicts off the street covered in ink and swearing at each other all day (if I'm a husband and my wife stays at home, am I comfortable with her being there alone with these guys?)

2. Owner/Personality. This type of video features the owner of the business, or a sales manager if he/she is more comfortable in front of the camera. No matter who you decide to use, it is important that the majority of your videos feature that person. They become the "face" of your company to the community. Again, some tips:

- These can be a little longer, depending on the subject matter. 60 to 120 seconds is a good length, unless you are demonstrating something that take longer and is interesting to the potential viewer.

- Focus on subjects that will have meaning to someone looking for a roofing contractor. Do not shoot platitude filled "commercials" about how you are the 'best in town.' It's fine to ask for their business, but give them a compelling reason to take the next step in the sales process with you.

- Feature other members of the team, especially as you develop a good size library of videos. For example, Mary in accounting is having her 20th anniversary with the company this month. Do a short video introducing Mary and acknowledging her long service. This type of video will show people a more human side of your business.

- Some of these should be shot "in the field," others "in the studio." Proper planning in advance will result in a library of videos that are meaningful to a prospect and generate interest in your company.

3. "On The Roof." This genre of video is where you demonstrate potential issues that a homeowner might face with proper roof inspection and maintenance. These videos are powerful generators of trust, and do a great job of establishing you as an expert who is willing to share their knowledge. Some subject ideas:

- Tips for doing an annual roof inspection
- Gutter cleaning, how to do it properly and why it's important
- Chimney inspection tips

- Flashing, valley work, working with skylights...almost anything that you encounter in the regular course of replacing roofs is a good subject for a short video.
- If you do "job progress" videos, replacing the flashing next to the chimney for example. Don't expect someone to watch a 30 minute video of you doing the job. Plan to do a lot of editing after the video is shot, or shoot short sequences with narration during the job.
- Be sure to include a "safety disclaimer" at the start of every video. You don't want to be sued by a homeowner who watched your video, tried the job themselves, and had an accident.

See, it's a lot easier than you may have thought to come up with good subjects. In the next section I'll share with you how to convert these ideas into top quality videos

How to Get Started Producing Quality Videos for Your Business

When I talk with clients about video they immediately assume they'll need a lot of expensive equipment or have to hire a specialist to produce them. Not the case anymore. To begin producing quality videos that will show your company in a positive light you only need two things: some basic equipment and a video plan.

When I say basic equipment I would bet that you already have the most important piece, the camera. That's right, if you have a relatively recent smart phone, either an iPhone or an Android, you already have a camera that will give you quality raw video footage. There are those who say that one format is better than another. Honestly, I can't tell the difference between a finished video that was shot on an iPhone from one that was taken with an

Android. So whichever one you own, use it.

As you begin to produce more video content, you may want to add some additional equipment. If you are going to create video in a room in your office, you will want a "green screen" background. Without going into a lot of videographer jargon, this is a solid color that you stand in front of when shooting the video. This neutral color will help your viewer focus on the subject of the video, you or the props you are demonstrating. Using very simple video production software (you probably already have this) it is an easy matter to superimpose your video over another background, like outdoors or on a roof, by replacing the "green screen" digitally.

You can search online for a photographers supply company and buy a fabric green screen and the rack system to support it, but that's not necessary. You can buy sheets of material from a fabric store and create your own. Even simpler is to head over to the hardware store and buy a gallon of dinosaur green paint in the kids section and paint one wall. (Make sure it is a smooth wall, not textured, or you will not be able to light it easily.)

A tripod to hold your phone/camera steady when shooting is important. Since your phone is lightweight, you don't need to invest in a heavy professional style tripod. Most phones have an adaptor that they fit in that will mount into the tripod's quick release. Or there are holders that you phone will slip into that can be attached to the tripod. You may have to go online to find this.

For indoor shooting having control of the light is important. You want to eliminate shadows cast by the subject against the background. Here again you can go to a photographers supply company and buy studio lights. Alien Bees is a company that manufactures a very inexpensive but accurate studio lighting, we use them in our indoor studio. But you don't need to go to that level. I've seen great video produced using the halogen shop lights you can get at Home Depot or Lowes for less than $50. You'll have to experiment with distance from the subject since these do not have the light intensity adjustments of regular photographers studio lights.

Most important is sound quality. Your viewers will overlook average video quality, but if they have to struggle to hear what is being said they will click away in seconds. Invest some money in a good quality wireless microphone. You can expect to pay around $125 for a system that will synch into your phone/camera. Do not try to skip this expense. Whether you do most of your videos indoors or outside, good audio quality is critical.

A video editing software program will be necessary for any "studio" style videos you produce. Fortunately, you probably already have a good basic program. If you use a Windows based computer then Windows Movie Maker is already loaded and ready to use. For Mac users, iMovie is your included tool. Both are pretty intuitive, and have good help tools.

Another option are programs produced by TechSmith. They have a free program you can download, Jing, that will do screen capture videos of up to five minutes. For a more versatile, and complicated, solution consider their Camtasia product. This is a complete video editing platform that gives you total control over the finished product. You can upload video files from your phone for editing, or create longer screen captures. We also use this program in our office to produce video webinars. The retail cost for Camtasia is about $250.

That's it. With those equipment basics you are ready to be the Steven Spielberg for your company. To produce quality videos that accurately represent the good name of your company you need more than just equipment. You'll also need a plan to create engaging videos that will hold the interest of your prospects. Here are some tips for how to do that:

1. Quality videos don't happen by accident. They're created with pre-production planning. The following are a must:

- Shot list. Take a legal pad and write down the different shots you want to include in your video. It may only be one or two for a short video, but plan them
- Story board. Make a simple sketch of any complex shots or transitions between shots. This is especially important if you're shooting at a job site.
- Prop list per scene. A professional looking finished product will be the result if you have everything you're going to need ready before starting the camera.
- B-roll. This is additional footage that will make your story come to life when it comes time to edit. Some examples might include showing your crew getting ready at the start of the job, you driving to a job site and talking to the camera held by one of your people in the passenger seat, walking around your building with equipment and activity in the background as you answer common questions.

2. Be clear and give a reason to stick around. Make sure viewers know in the first five to 10 seconds exactly why they should keep watching. Tell them, and show them the benefits they'll get from watching your video. Even for a short, 45 to 90 second video, have an attention getting headline as you begin. People have very

short attention spans when sitting in front of their computers.

3. Be Energetic. People who demonstrate passion and energy on camera are more likely to hold a viewer's attention than being monotone and dull. Just watch any stand-up comedian and see how his or her energy affects an audience.

Try speaking a bit louder than normal and be a little more animated with your body language. Don't mumble. Look at the camera when appropriate, at the work you are demonstrating, and then back at the camera.

All this might feel strange in front of the camera, but can create a more engaging video. It may take a little practice, but is worth the time.

4. Safety First. If you do videos at a jobsite or on a roof, emphasize safety. Mention the importance of a properly set ladder, using safety blocks or a harness on the roof, wearing proper foot ware. Make certain that any of your crew that might be in the background are using safety best practices.

5. Post production. Once you have your video footage shot, what do you do with it? In some cases, like "on the job" testimonials from customers, they are ready to go without any post production work. Other times you will want to load the .mp4 file into your editing software and make adjustments as needed.

If you decide to make video an important part of your company marketing then you'll want to have an intro and outro created. An intro is a short, 10 seconds or less, clip that "brands" your company and your channel. An outro is another clip that typically shows your company name, phone number, and website address.

Every video you produce should have the intro and outro added as a part of your post production work. I have talked about Fiverr.com elsewhere in this book, that is a good place to look for someone to create short video clips for you.

Once you have your videos created and produced, then next step is to upload them to your channel on the key video sites on the internet.

How To Create Your YouTube Channel

Producing a library of marketing videos is the first step, now you need a place for prospects to find and watch them. Enter YouTube, Vimeo, Daily Motion, Hulu, and a host of other websites that are designed to display video. The best way to combine making your videos available along with enhancing your company brand is to create a channel on these sites. I'm going to talk about YouTube, but the process is similar with the other sites.

How many sites do you need? Really, just one: YouTube. It is the second largest search engine in the world, based on number of searches conducted. The last statistics I read indicated that YouTube controlled almost 85% of the online video marketplace. The value in also creating a channel and posting your videos to one or two other sites is that the search engine spiders do crawl them, and there is page rank value in being found on multiple sites. We use an automated video posting software program for our clients, but still only upload videos to three of the sites (YouTube, Vimeo, Daily Motion.)

Creating a YouTube channel is an easy process you should be able to complete is less than a half hour. The best advice I can suggest is to do a Google search for, "how to create a YouTube channel for my business." Then look at the publishing date of all the links that come up to find the most recent. I say this because the process changes fairly often, especially as Google continues to integrate their various tools and programs. (If you didn't know, Google owns YouTube.) Ironically, you should be able to find a YouTube video showing you how to create a channel on YouTube.

Strategies For Marketing Your Videos

Once you've created your Video Channel, here are some best practices for using it as a marketing tool.

1. How should I organize my video content?

Instead of presenting your videos in a single long list, group them into playlists by topic or theme. Some topics might include: Customer Testimonials, "On The Roof," Our Company, etc. With a little navigation, viewers can more easily find videos that interest them.

2. How often should I post videos?

Upload new videos as often as your schedule and budget allow, especially as you are getting started. Once you have a library of a dozen or more in your channel, you might create a publishing schedule and then announce on your website and through social media every time you publish a new video.

3. How do I customize my channel background?

When designing your YouTube channel try to mirror your

company's existing online look, including the color schemes and logos on your website. You can choose a background color for your channel and then upload your background image. This congruence will help establish your brand in the local market.

4. Should I upload commercials about my products and services?

People come to YouTube to be entertained, educated and informed, but not to watch commercials. The idea is to put helpful, informative videos on YouTube that enhance your company's image without being overly promotional. It is good to have a call to action, that is one of the reasons to add an outro slide to every video. That slide should have your company name, address, phone number, and website address. Leave the outro slide in view for the last five to ten seconds of your video.

5. How should I describe and tag my videos?

When you upload an mp4 file to YouTube their software will format it to YouTube standards and create a unique identifier, like a URL, for that video. Once the video is available on YouTube you want to optimize by adding a title, description, and tags. The title should be the subject of the video, for example: Chimney Flashing. I also like to add the company name and phone number if they both will fit into the space allowed. So a title might look like this: Chimney Flashing, Smith Roofing, 555-555-1212.

The video description is a place to let the potential viewer know more about what the video is about, as well as list your company contact information. Using appropriate keywords for your business is important, but generally no more than three of your keywords in each description. At the time I'm writing this you are allowed up to 600 characters in the description box. I always try to fill the box with relevant information.

YouTube has 'spiders' that crawl all video content just like the search engines have spiders that crawl all the pages of a website. There are different opinions as to how much of the description box these spiders crawl. Some believe it is only the first two sentences, others say the entire area. When I'm writing video descriptions I split the difference. That is, I make sure the first two sentences are carefully worded and include my most important keywords for that video. Then I write the rest of the sentences to get as close as possible to the 600 character limit. I always like to include the website address and telephone number somewhere near the bottom of the description.

The "Tags" area under the description box is where you can put a series of keywords. I like to include a location with some of these, like Roofing Contractor Albuquerque. You also want to include keywords that are relevant to the subject of the video. For example, if you're posting an on-the-job video showing chimney repair, add keyword tags like "chimney," "chimney repair," "flashing" "chimney cap" and "roof repair." That way searchers can easily find it via search engines and YouTube search.

When optimizing your video you'll also see a tab for "Advanced." Most people do not complete this area, but YouTube values the information and uses it in search placement, so I always complete it. Here is how I enter information on this page.

Comments: I check this to allow comments, and allow all except potentially inappropriate comments, with the newest first.

Users can view ratings: I check this.

License and Rights: Standard YouTube license. This protects your content from other using some or all in their own videos.

Caption Certification: I always select the first option. If your video has been used on television you will choose another.

Distribution Options: I check both of these.

Age restrictions: I do not check this.

Category: I use Education or People and Blogs.

Video Location: this is very important! Enter your office address so that your videos will be 'geo-tagged' by YouTube.

Video Language: English (assuming it is in English)

Community Contributions: Do not check this box.

Recording Date: Enter the date the video was made, or the upload date.

Video Statistics: I do not check this box.

Content Declaration: I do not use paid placements in my videos, so I do not check this box.

This may seem like extra work that doesn't really impact the potential customer who is watching the video, but it may help get your video placed higher in the search results. A completely optimized video will also be offered more frequently by YouTube than one that is not properly optimized.

6. Should I allow comments on my videos?

Allowing people to comment on your videos should encourage them to share their experiences with your brand and show that you're open to feedback. You can automatically display comments, display them only after you've approved them or keep them hidden. If you enable comments, you still have the option to delete any that are inappropriate or spammy.

Just like Facebook and other social media sites, the comments section is where you directly interact with and engage your community. If you allow comments realize that it's important to respond in the most helpful and authentic way possible, which means someone in your company is going to have to monitor your channel(s) regularly.

7. How should I promote my channel?

Every time you upload a new video, share a direct link to it across all of your business's social media networks. You can embed your YouTube videos and playlists in your business's website or blog.

You can also try to build an audience for your videos with Google Adwords for video, which lets you create and manage video promotions on YouTube and elsewhere online. Google Adwords campaigns are cost-per-view (CPV). To set a CPV bid, you enter the highest price you want to pay. For example, if you think it's worth 25 cents for someone to watch your video, set that amount as your maximum CPV. Then you pay only when people watch your video.

8. How can I measure my channel's success?

YouTube offers a free, self-service viewership analytics and reporting tool called YouTube Analytics. It tells you how many people watch your videos, how often, and how they discovered your videos.

YouTube Analytics also shows you how many subscribers you have, as well as how many likes, dislikes, comments and shares each video has received. Tracking which videos are most popular, along with the precise moment people stop watching them, can help you learn which types of content resonate with your viewers.

WHAT TO DO NOW:

1. Decide to incorporate video into your marketing! No matter what else you do to promote your company, video is that important in today's internet.

2. Plan your video campaigns.
   a. Who in your company has a smart phone?

   b. Do you have a place in your office to shoot indoor videos? What is needed to set this up properly? Who will get it done?

   c. What type(s) of videos do you want to have in your library? How many? By what date?

   d. Does someone on your team know how to use the post production software you have? Assign learning this to two people (in case one leaves.)

3. Set Video Marketing goals.
   a. When will you have your first "customer testimonial" live.

b. When will your YouTube channel be ready for uploads?

4. Assign a manager to this task. It is rare that an owner or key managers will have the time to follow through on the set up tasks and ongoing monitoring of your video marketing program. Put someone in charge. It doesn't have to be a full time employee. With a little bit of searching you should be able to find a high school or community college student interested in video and looking for "real world" experience.

Pay Per Click--The Best Way to Get on Page One

Paid search engine advertising is one of the most common marketing strategies employed by roofing companies. It can also be one of the biggest wastes of your valuable marketing budget if not managed correctly. Even those companies that retain the services of a paid advertising manager may not be achieving the best return on investment. If you as the owner aren't conversant with how to correctly set up and monitor a paid advertising campaign, how would you know?

In this chapter I want to answer several of frequently asked questions we hear when talking with roofing contractors about paid search. These include:

- What is Paid Search Advertising?
- What are the benefits of using paid search for a roofing company?
- How do I begin if I want to start a paid advertising campaign?
- What is a Quality Score, and how is it calculated?
- How do I write an effective ad?
- Why do I need Landing Pages?
- 5 Mistakes to Avoid in your paid search campaigns
- Can I hire someone to manage this for me? How do I do that?

My purpose is to give you enough information so that you can know the right questions to ask, whether you decide to have someone on your team supervise your paid ad campaigns or you retain the services of an outside company. Keep in mind that search engine advertising is dynamic. That is, change is the rule and not the exception. If you decide to invest a sizeable percentage of your marketing budget in paid search you must also commit to a consistent program of testing and learning.

Let's get started.

What is Paid Search Advertising?

For this discussion I'm going to refer to all types of paid search advertising using the acronym "PPC." PPC stands for *pay-per-click* and refers to the type of search engine marketing where an advertiser pays a fee each time one of their ads is clicked. Essentially, it's a way of buying visits to your site, rather than attempting to "earn" those visits organically.

Most paid search is done using the three major search engines; Google, Bing, and Yahoo. For simplicity sake I'm going to use "Google" as a generic reference to these search engines. (Google currently controls 70% of the search market.) There is also a strategy that can be done with an Adwords account that allows you as an advertiser to place your ad on websites that you believe will be visited by prospects for your roofing service. This strategy is not typically used by roofing contractors, and I will not be talking about it at all.

A PPC advertising program is quite simple to begin. You create an account with the search engines, an "Adwords" account as Google names it. Your account is funded with a credit card. Then you place an advertisement that is tied to the keywords that you believe your prospects will search. Every time your ad is clicked, sending a visitor to your website or a landing page, you have to pay the search engine a small fee. When PPC is working correctly, the fee is trivial, because *the visit is worth more than what you pay for it.* In other words, if we pay $36 for a click, but the click results in a $12,000 roofing job, then you've made a hefty profit.

A lot goes into building a winning PPC campaign: from researching and selecting the right keywords, to organizing those keywords into well-structured campaigns and ad groups, to setting up PPC landing pages that are optimized for conversions. Search engines reward advertisers who can create relevant, intelligently targeted pay-per-click campaigns by charging them less for ad clicks. If your ads and landing pages are useful and satisfying to users, Google charges you less per click, leading to higher profits for your business. If you want to start using PPC, it's important to learn how to do it right.

PPC marketing is not limited to the search engines. Social media sites like Facebook and Instagram also accepts ads. If you are considering a PPC program give careful consideration to these channels. Here are some reasons why. First, Facebook ad costs are generally lower than a corresponding ad on Google, Bing, or Yahoo. Second, because Facebook collects so much data on its users, you can be quite specific in who you display your ad to. Third, the Facebook dashboard for ad management is quite intuitive and easy to use. Fourth, split testing of your ads (comparing the results of one ad against a second ad) is less complicated. Fifth, because Facebook is allowing you to direct where your ad is placed, there is not the Quality Score challenge that is part of search engine advertising.

The down side of advertising on Facebook is that someone who is shopping for a roofing contractor is not as likely to go to Facebook looking for one. Your ad must interrupt the prospect as they are on the site, and lead them to a landing page that is compelling enough for them to call you.

What are the benefits of using paid search for a roofing company?

PPC campaigns have numerous benefits, including: measurability, payment for performance, timing, control, bidding, speed to market and targeting.

Here are a few examples of how PPC can help you achieve specific business goals:

Generate new leads: Use PPC to obtain new prospects and gather information about their needs over time. You can drive new prospects to a special landing page on your website where they can sign up for a free demo or download a new report or free content.

Direct Sales: Drive new leads to a transaction page

Build Brand awareness: Use PPC to invite prospects to an event, either on or offline, or to promote something newsworthy.

Immediate measurement: Use a true pay-for-performance marketing medium to allow you to quickly determine whether your campaign is profitable or not.

Pay for performance: You only pay for actual clicks to your listing. If a user enters a search term, sees your site and clicks the listing, it is because s/he believes your listing will provide the info s/he wants.

Control what visitors see on your site; focus the conversation: You can direct traffic to specific pages on your site. You should develop landing pages for each campaign, pages offering specific information and a strong call to action.

Excellent timing: You bid on the search terms/keywords used by your prospects when they are searching for info on the web.

Bid what a prospect is worth: You can input different bid amounts on keywords to reflect how valuable the leads are for you. For example, you may bid on a very specific phrase such as, "Roofing Contractor, Portland," and pay more for those clicks because they are more valuable to you than general keywords that may drive a greater volume of less targeted traffic.

Limit Your Spending: You can choose a maximum bid level for each click, as well as a total spend you are willing to make each day. This way you only spend what those website visits are worth to you.

Speed to market: You can launch a paid search campaign as soon as your website is live, building immediate traffic that may take months to generate organically.

Develop Targeted Campaigns: You can develop very specific campaigns that include seasonality, regionality, and other factors that influence the purchasing decision.

How do I begin if I want to start a paid advertising campaign?

Before you can implement search engine marketing best practices it is important that you understand who the players are in every PPC transaction that occurs. Most of us who have spent money on advertising in the past believe that we are a priority for the vendor of the ad space or airtime or whatever marketing venue we invested in. *That is not the case with PPC advertising.*

There are three interrelated entities that are in constant tension in any PPC account. Most Adwords users have a good understanding of the marketing channel from a micro point of view. That is, how to get into and work on their personal account. What they fail to understand is the conceptual framework of a PPC account, and the important relationships involved.

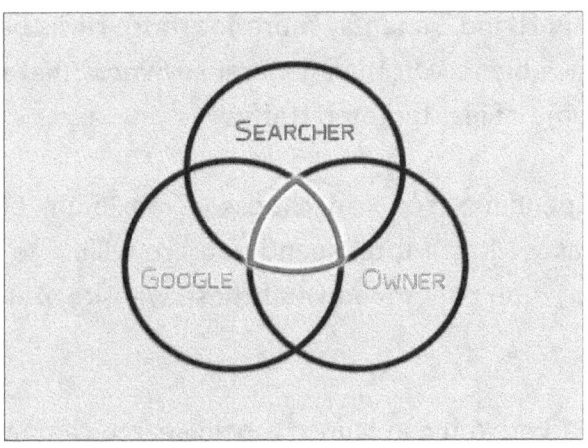

Here are the three entities that are a part of every PPC transaction: the "Searcher," the AdWords account "Owner," and Google. Let's briefly analyze each of these, and then look at why a thorough understanding of this concept can save you thousands of dollars on your own campaigns.

The Searcher: this is the person looking for products and services online who types a search inquiry into the Google (or any search engine) search box. *Google considers the Searcher to be their primary customer*, and constructs their algorithms to help searchers easily and accurately find what they are looking for. Part of helping the Searcher is providing paid ads relevant to their keywords. Google has extensively studied user eye movement and selection tendencies, and will "reward" well written and properly structured PPC campaigns with better placement on the page and a lower cost per click.

While an advertiser is the source of cash flow, Searchers are the lifeblood of any search engine. Without these tens of millions of searches each day Google would quickly wither up and die. As an advertiser we can never assume that we are more important to the search engines than the Searcher; the Searcher controls the PPC world.

The Owner: This refers to the person who creates an AdWords account and uses the PPC marketing channel to sell their product or service to the Searcher. The Owner is also a customer of Google's, but in the overall scheme of things, takes a back seat in terms of importance.

The search engines place a lot of emphasis for Owner's to comply with detailed regulations that sometimes seem illogical from an advertising point of view. Remember, these rules are in place to protect the Searcher from any owner misconduct or misleading advertising. Google will always err on the side of protecting the Searcher. The onus falls on the Owner to comply with these policies and rules. Failure to do so may get you "slapped," or banned from advertising on the Google platform.

The Owner must learn to think like the potential Searcher. What words is a searcher likely to type into the search bar in their favorite search engine to help them find your products or services? (By the way, owners of an AdWords account have analysis tools that will help them know what keywords Searchers are typing in.) By incorporating those words into the "headline" of your ad, you enhance the experience for the Searcher, and in the process earn a higher "Quality Score" from the search engine.

It is this Quality Score that determines where your ad is placed on the page, and the cost per click you pay.

Here is the ongoing challenge for any advertiser using PPC: creating advertisements that are compelling enough for Searchers to click, that comply with Google's best practices, and which you are constantly testing to improve and in the process lower your advertising cost.

Google: or any search engine. We've seen that Google has two customers: the Searcher and the Owner. While Google wants both of its customers to be happy using the AdWords platform, it is also in business to make a profit. If you carefully analyze the results of the default settings for an PPC account you'll see that many are set up to help a PPC client spend more money. As you develop a longer track record with Google as an advertiser, they will offer you ideas for how to utilize more of the platforms capabilities (that is, spend more money.) You may also be assigned a customer service rep who will contact you directly with suggestions and proposals. What you will never hear from Google are ideas of how you can spend less. They are a profit driven company, and AdWords is their primary profit generator.

It falls to the Owner be aware of how to manage a campaign that is generating the highest return on investment for the dollars being spent on PPC, while at the same time following the rules created to protect the Searcher.

Failure to understand the "big picture" of PPC can cost you a great deal of money, and possibly even get you banned from the platform. Failure to "see" with the eyes of your prospect, and adjust your campaigns accordingly, can cause a total disconnect between you and your potential client.

For you as the Owner, the goal of a well run PPC campaign is to understand both the Searcher and Google enough to maximize results at the lowest possible cost. It is not a "set it and forget it" program.

The PPC Auction

The actual transaction of someone going to the search engine, typing in their query, and then being taken to a page that includes a variety of paid ads is a complicated auction process that occurs in milliseconds. Here's how it works.

It all begins with the Searcher entering their inquiry terms. When they do that Google looks at the available pool of advertisers and determines whether there will be an auction. If more than one advertiser is bidding on keywords that *Google deems relevant to the search query*, an auction is triggered. Keep in mind that keywords are not search queries. Specific keywords may be entered into auctions for a wide range of search queries, depending on the match type you have specified in your advertising account.

What gets entered into these auctions? Advertisers identify keywords they want to bid on, how much they are willing to spend, and create groupings of these keywords that are paired with ads. Google then enters the keyword from your account that it deems to be most relevant into the auction with the maximum bid you've specified as well as the ad that is associated with that keyword.

Here is where the confusion begins. Which ads appear on the page for the Searcher, where do they show up on the page, and how much are you charged if your ad is selected? Actually, it is not that mysterious. Once you are entered into the auction,

Google looks at two key factors to determine where your ad ranks: your maximum bid and your quality score. (We'll look at Quality Score in detail in just a minute.)

The auction formula is this: Ad Rank (where your ad appears on the page) = Your Maximum Bid x Your Quality Score.

The cost of your ad, if yours is selected by the Searcher, is calculated like this:

Your Price = The Ad Rank of the Person Below You / Your Quality Score + $0.01

It is commonly believed that the company who has the first ad at the top of the page is paying more than any other ad on the page. The second ad is paying the second most, etc. As you can see from the formula, this is not necessarily true. The key variable is your quality score.

What is a Quality Score, and how is it calculated?

Do you want to know the secret to dramatically lower your cost to acquire a new customer when using Google AdWords? It's simple: improve your Quality Score! Based on a study completed using combined data from thousands of Pay Per Click campaigns run in the second half of 2017, and representing just over $100 million in annual spend, we can calculate a current idea of just how much impact Quality Score can have.

Here's the bottom line: for every Quality Score point above the average of 5 out of 10, your Cost Per Acquisition will drop by an average of 16%. Conversely, for every Quality Score point below the average of 5/10, your CPA will increase by 16%.

It is an oversimplification to say that the most important metric you should be looking at when managing your company's

AdWords advertising is Quality Score, but understanding the components of Quality Score and focusing attention on improving where you can has a definite impact on your return on investment.

In Google's mind, Quality Score matters because it represents the relevance of your ads to their customers search queries. Calculating and assigning a quality score to your advertising is one of the primary ways that Google maintains its status as the most used search engine. It helps Google ensure that the ads searchers are seeing are relevant to their inquiry. Both Bing and Yahoo have developed a similar metric to provide their users with the most relevant search results.

Here's the bottom line: Quality Score affects your account success. If your keyword level Quality Score is low, your keyword might not even be entered into an auction. That means you ad won't show at all, you'd have no chance to complete for business. If your Quality Score is low, your ad rank will be low, driving less traffic to your site, at a higher price, and reducing your ROI.

There are actually seven types of quality scores. "Seven types??" you might be saying. Most active users of PPC know about the Quality Score that is associated with the individual keywords in their account, also known as the "visible level Quality Score." What fewer users are aware of is the fact that Google calculates a variety of Quality Scores. How they are weighed with and against each other, and their combined impact on your account, remains shrouded in mystery. We can be certain that they were designed to help Google with one or both of its primary mandates: provide the best quality search experience for its customers and do everything possible to maximize Google's income.

Here are the seven distinct types of Quality Scores that we have been able to determine.

1. **Account-Level Quality Score**. This score is the calculated result of the historical performance of all keywords and ads in an account. If you have a large number of low Quality Score keywords and low click through rate ads with poor historical performance in your account, your QS will remain low. This makes it difficult to introduce new keywords and ads, and they will start at this lower quality score.

2. **Ad Group Quality Score**. This is a way to determine which areas you need to work on within a campaign. Let's say you have an ad group with a low keyword Quality Score, but your overall average is a 7. You have another ad group with an average of 4. This makes it clear where you should devote your attention, working on your lowest average Quality Score areas first leads to a better return on investment.

3. **Keyword Level Quality Score**. This score is visible in your AdWords interface, and is the QS that Google assigns to your keywords. It is a scale of 1 to 10, with 1 being poor and 10 fantastic. It is calculated by the performance of search queries that exactly match your keyword.

4. **Ad Level Quality Score**. The individual ads that you are running in each of your ad groups will have a different click through rate, which determines the overall ad level Quality Score. If you have a lot of low CTR ads in an ad group, this could be a contributing factor to a low Quality Score since AdWords considers all of your ads when calculating your

scores.

5. **Landing Page Quality Score**. Google has three priorities for evaluating a landing page: relevant and original content, transparency, and navigability. Google consciously attempts to force advertisers into making quality websites that its users will find useful and relevant.

6. **Display Network Quality Score**. Unless you are using the Google Display Network this is not relevant. Roofing companies would not normally use this network.

7. **Mobile Quality Score**. In the past 24 months mobile searches have grown geometrically. One recent study indicated that 70% of all searches on Google originated from a mobile device. This trend begs the question: how does Google incorporate mobile into Quality Score calculations? In April of 2017 Google made it official. Search results will now be presented giving preference to mobile friendly websites. This extends to a PPC campaign because when someone clicks on your ad they will be taken to a landing page or a page on your website. If these are not "mobile friendly" in design and formatting for the mobile platforms then your ad will not be presented as frequently, and they will cost you more per click.

I've gone into more detail about Quality Scores than you might be interested in, but it is that important. Particularly for the business owner who is tasked with managing their own campaign, a correct understanding of Quality Score can be the difference between a profitable program and one that is a waste of valuable time and money.

How Do I Write an Effective PPC Ad?

Writing ad copy for PPC can be a tough feat. The good news is, you don't have to be a super-creative copywriter to whip up competitive ad text. In fact, following a pragmatic approach can be advantageous.

Here are a few simple steps that will help you to assess the competitive landscape and write ad copy that will stand out against your competitors' regardless of your ad rank.

1. Do competitive research. What are other roofing contractors who use PPC saying in their ads? Most of the time their "headline" will be their company name or a platitude about "best roofer". Unless you've also spent a great deal of money on radio and TV over a period of years, most homeowners looking for a roofing contractor will not recognize your company name. Since everyone says they're the "best roofer" that is meaningless to a prospect.

Also realize that many of the paid ads will not be for other roofing companies. Companies like Home Advisors, Yellow Pages, Angie's List and other companies that offer consumers a listing of companies spend a lot on PPC ads. Without anything else to go on, many searchers will choose one of these.

To stand out your ad has to catch attention. Do you have a slogan or value proposition? Use it as a headline. We did some work for a roof repair company who had a great tagline: "Think you need a new roof? Think again!" It became a great headline for their PPC campaign ads. The point is, be different, stand out and you'll get more clicks.

2. Identify Your Differentiating Characteristic. Now that you've assessed the competition, use your knowledge to become the leader of the pack. Consider your page-mates' ad copy and identify a differentiator that will make you stand out. This is your opportunity to sell yourself! Tell the searcher why you are providing them a better product or deal than your competitors.

Maybe it's your years in the marketplace, or top ranking from the BBB, or your company was selected for an industry award. Anything that might attract attention and prompt a Searcher to read your ad.

3. Include A Call To Action. To complete your ad, include a call to action that gives your searchers an incentive to click. You can opt for the standard "call us now," but if you really want to step it up a notch, consider a more creative alternative. If you have a high profile past client (and get their permission) say something like "Coach Smith trusted his roof to us, you should too." Make an offer that gives something of value to a homeowner: "Free roof emergency kit with every estimate."

4. Use Ad Extensions. Extensions are a way to increase the size of your ad at no additional cost. There are several types of extensions you can utilize. Among them are call extensions, sitelink extensions, location extensions, offer extensions, and application extensions (for people using a tablet or mobile phone to search.)

5. Watch Your Metrics. Your ad may be complete, but you're not finished yet. Let it get a few impressions and then assess your success! It's tough to predict the performance of a new ad, so ad copy testing is critical. Often the ad copy you thought would win out ends up losing. There's no way to know what will work until you test ads against each other.

Why Do I Need Landing Pages?

The classic mistake that far too many roofing contractors make when starting a new PPC campaign is sending someone who clicks on their ad directly to their website, usually to the home page. "What's wrong with that," you're asking? While you may have an award winning homepage that was designed by a well known internet guru who charged you a lot of money, but it may not be at all relevant to the reason someone is searching for you.

Your PPC ad is written for a specific response. It is crafted to speak to a specific need in mind of the Searcher. Your website is a more general introduction to your company and all of its products/services. It may not immediately speak to the need in the mind of the prospect. A landing page is a "single page website" that does.

Why does someone need what you offer? What, specifically, are they looking for when they go to a search engine and type in their keywords? That is the question you want to answer for them immediately when they click on your ad. The way you do this is with a Landing Page. A Landing Page is just what it sounds like, an online page that specifically addresses the exact question the searcher is asking. Let me give you an example.

There has been a heavy storm in your area, and the rain continues to fall. Mrs. Jones sees water dripping through the ceiling in her dining room right where her chandelier is attached. And not just a little drip...it's more of a small stream. After moving the dining room table out of the way, she goes to her computer and

Google's "emergency roof repair." That just happens to be one of your specialties, and a keyword you use in one of your PPC ads. Mrs. Jones clicks on your ad and is directed to your home page. There she learns that you have been in business for more than 20 years, do roof repairs and replacements, have great crews who wear clean uniforms, and a whole lot of information that is not relevant to her immediate need. She gets frustrated and goes back to Google to find someone who answers her question.

If, when she clicked on your ad she had been taken to a landing page with just a few facts that were directly related to her question, you would have gotten the business. What did Mrs. Jones need in that moment? All she needed to see was your company name, a bold headline talking about 24/7 emergency service, and in large type the phone number you want her to call. Anything else is irrelevant to her at that moment. Make sense? **Think like your prospect!**

We call this strategy **"One Decision Marketing"** because it is focused on helping a prospect make the one decision that is most relevant to them at that time. Here's another advantage to using landing pages. Remember Google's primary interest in making sure that all of its search customers find what they need quickly and easily? The Google algorithms track search behavior and grade your ads and site based on how people react to them. If, in the example of Mrs. Jones, she had clicked on your ad, gone to a landing page and stopped her search, Google will interpret that as she found exactly what she needed. Kudos to you! Because she went back and searched again, it is obvious she didn't get what she needed from your site. Not good! Your quality score is affected by her search behavior.

When I explain this to prospects and clients a common question is, "does that mean I need a landing page for each ad I run?" No, not each individual ad, but a landing page for each product or service you are marketing. You may have several ads, each ad has specific keywords and therefore a specific want or need that it is addressing, but are all focused on bringing prospects to a particular product or service. These ads should all be directed to a specific landing page so that a prospective customer has their immediate questions answered.

Let me say it another way. In your roofing company you replace residential roofs. You also do gutter and downspout work, and also bid on commercial roofs. Each of these areas of specialization might have three or five or even more keyword phrases that are commonly typed in by Searchers. Each of those keyword phrases can have one or more specific ads ("more" because you are constantly testing to improve your results). All of those ads will link to one landing page that has relevant information to that specific specialty of your company, and a clear call to action so the Searcher knows exactly what you want them to do next. Make sense?

If you are just sending prospects to your home page you are losing business as well as hurting your Quality Score. This costs you money!

5 Pay Per Click Mistakes That Could Be Costing You Money

If you currently have active PPC campaigns as a part of your marketing spend each month, see if you are committing any of these "PPC Sins."

1. Trusting the "default" setting in your AdWords account

If you read the last few paragraphs you better understand that while Google is in the business of providing services to you as an advertiser, their primary motivation is to make the maximum profit they can from every account. There is nothing wrong with that, but you don't want to spend your money without extracting the maximum return on investment possible.

Here's the Rule: It's Your Money—Maximize Your Return on Investment!

Many new and even experienced PPC users do not evaluate just how the default settings in AdWords can impact their expense. You should turn off any setting that will not optimize your ad spend. For example, the default setting for "content network" is on. This means that your ads will be shown on sites like About.com and The New York Times (and you will pay for the curious who click, whether they have an interest in your product or not.)

Will advertising in those venues help you sell your products or services? In most cases no. You want your ads to show up for people who are directly searching for what you offer (we call this the "search network") and not on secondary and even tertiary sites.

2. Confusing "Clicks" with Profits

What we're really going to talk about here is conversion metrics and the importance of closely monitoring the statistics for each ad that you have running. Peter Drucker, the "man who invented management" once said: "what gets measured, gets managed." That is so true when it comes to pay per click. There are quite a few variables, so let me try to sort through them and give you some suggestions to improve your results.

Here's the Rule: "Click through" is good…"Conversion" is better!

The most obvious measure of a PPC campaign is the percentage of time that a searcher will click on your ad. If you get one click for every 2500 times your ad is displayed, you have a low click through rate. If you're getting one for every 5 times—you're a genius! But keep in mind that the click-through rate is useless by itself. It will have a significant impact on the cost of your campaign—you're paying per click, remember?—but it tells you nothing about the benefits you get in return.

The bottom line in any pay per click campaign is how well the ad spend generates income. Every decision you make in any campaign should be focused on getting customers to spend money with you, not just click on the ad. That could mean that an ad that is generating a huge number of clicks should be pulled because those prospects are not converting to customers. By the way, this same evaluation should be done for each keyword you choose to bid on.

One of the biggest advantages to online advertising is the ability to calculate your return on investment. The water gets a little muddied when you also have off line marketing programs, seasonal variations in your business, or an existing online sales flow when starting a new PPC program. Fortunately, there are quite a few number of tools to help you measure your progress.

At the most basic level, you should set up and pay close attention to Google's conversion tracking tools. They are designed to help you determine the rate at which people who go to your site from an ad actually do something specific; like make a purchase or ask for more information or sign up for a mailing list. Capturing an online sale is obviously the best indication that your PPC investment is paying off. But if you have a more complicated sales pipeline, one that includes both on and offline marketing, determining the value of a click can be more difficult.

Google's tools can be accessed by going to the "Reporting and Tools" menu in your AdWords account and selecting "Conversions." There is a setup wizard that will guide you through the process. These tools will enable you to tell Google what the different types of click on your site are worth to you, making a more accurate calculation of return on investment possible.

There are also many third party analysis tools and analysis service providers in the market that will help you measure and analyze your site. Some of these can be quite extensive in the amount of data they collect, and will have a fee structure that reflects this. For the typical roofing business, properly utilizing the basic Google tools will give you the data you need to make good business decisions.

3. Set it and Forget it

For people who are not familiar with just how dynamic the search engines are, and how frequently algorithms change, there is a temptation to identify some keywords and put a few ads out there and assume you'll continue to see good results. Even if you are making big bucks with pay per click, you must relentlessly evaluate and adjust. It is easy to do, carries very little risk, and has a huge potential upside.

Here's the Rule: "if it ain't broke, don't fix it" does not apply to PPC!

Do you think that a big search engine like Google is pretty stable? After all, they're the world's largest. Nope. In fact, in 2017 Google changed their algorithms 300 times (that they told us about). Think about it. That is more than once every business day of the year. Now not all of these changes will have a direct effect on pay per click, but certainly enough of them will that it behooves you to closely monitor your account results and be diligent about evaluating. The mantra "test-track-change" is adopted by all successful PPC managers.

Setting up A/B tests of ad headlines, landing pages, call to action phrases, and every other aspect of your campaigns should be the rule, not the exception. (An A/B test is where you measure the effect of changing one of these variables in an ad by running two ads that are identical except for the variable you are testing.) You should always be on the hunt for better keywords, better ads, and better ways to convert ad clickers. Even a small improvement in sales can make all the difference if it tips you into a positive return, because then you can start spending big and amplify those returns.

Here again, Google offers some helpful tools. A 'bid stimulator' gives you an indication of how well a new keyword might work for you. The 'campaign experiment' tool helps you divert a small portion of your budget to a parallel test, and then shift money over if it scores big or kill it if it's a bomb. Try campaigns on Bing, Yahoo and AOL.

Even after you have everything optimized and running smoothly and profitably, it is a good idea to take a step back every so often and see if there isn't some way to take it up to a higher level, or adapt to the ever changing conditions of the internet.

If all of this sounds like a lot of work, well, it is. On the other hand, a well designed and maintained pay per click campaign can be the single largest source of new customers for your roofing company.

4. Poor Money Management

With traditional advertising channels like radio, the newspaper, or yellow pages, it has always been difficult to know what is really producing revenue. Too often budget decisions were made based on what "feels right" or the size of your main competitors ad. That is a really bad way to budget for pay per click—you will almost certainly be throwing money away, or passing up the opportunity to really hit a home run.

Here's the Rule: If you're getting a positive ROI, base your budget on that and nothing else!

Using the tools I talked about earlier, you should be able to calculate with reasonable precision a return on your pay per click investment. The beauty of PPC is that it can be adjusted quickly. Little changes can provide big results. When you get great results and are making money, your know it is time to spend more. If you were earning two dollars for every dollar you spent, how many times would you repeat the behavior? Do this until you can't handle or just don't want the extra business, or until the monthly cash outlay becomes so large that it threatens to cause cash flow problems. Remember, an AdWords account is quite flexible, you can pause it at anytime.

5. Keyword Management

A related concept to poor money management is poor keyword management. Remember, you bid for keywords in an AdWords bid marketplace. If your keywords are not highly desired by other advertisers, you can get good ad placement for very little money. If you are selling an expensive service like roofing in a competitive marketplace, or a service with several other strong providers in your area who have more money to invest, you can be looking at bids of several hundred dollars per click on "hot keywords."

Here's The Rule: Find Your Best Keywords With Consistent Research and Constant Testing.

Here are three ideas you can try to keep your keywords relevant and costs down.

First, go local. This is a growing trend that first became popular about 18 months ago. What it means is that you append common search terms with your location. For example, "roofing contractor Dallas" or "roof repair Denver."

Second, focus on less obvious keywords, ideally ones that reflect your business specialties and strengths. An example might be something like "chimney repair" for a roofing firm that does tuck pointing, flashing and cap replacement on chimneys. This kind of call will often lead to more business.

Third, use negative keywords. This is a strategy that helps you insure that your ad is only being shown to people who are searching for what you actually offer. This is a simple strategy, but we constantly find that very few campaign managers employ it. The potential cost of overlooking this is in the thousands of dollars. Here are two simple examples that will make this clear.

1.   You are a roofing contractor and using AdWords to find new clients. Do you want your ad shown to someone looking for a job as a roofer? Of course not. Some good negative keywords for

your campaigns would be "career, careers, roofing careers, and roofing jobs." When Searchers typed in these words or phrases in their search, Google would not show your ad.

2.   Your business does not include commercial roofing. You would not like your ad to match a facilities manager who is soliciting bids for an office building so he might click on your ad. A good negative keyword in this case would be "commercial roofing."

Get the idea? Implementing this one strategy could dramatically improve your ROI.   Your AdWords account should be closely monitored to identify the words and phrases being used by potential clients. Once you have this data, it becomes a simple process of 'in with the good' and 'out with the bad.'

Can I Hire Someone to Do This For Me? How Do I Do That?

Managing a PPC program with multiple campaigns and ad groups takes both time and expertise. It is a specialized enough task that many contractors choose to outsource their Pay Per Click marketing. If that is something you want to explore then let me give you some tips for finding the right company.

1)   Make sure that the firm you are using has the technical ability to manage your account. Many times an ad agency will offer PPC management, but they turn your account over to outsource teams without knowing how to hire or manage the outsourcer. Often the people who are actually doing the day to day monitoring and managing of your account are not in the US. Another technique we've seen is firms that "macro manage" accounts. This means that your technical manager will make changes for accounts by grouping accounts rather than by making changes that are customized to your business--you become a

small fish in a big pond. Pick a management team with technical support that is big enough to be completive but small enough to manage your account like the VIP you are!

Google has a comprehensive certification program for PPC account managers. It requires a candidate to complete a training program, continuing education each year, and have experience managing individual accounts with a minimum monthly spend in excess of $10,000. Look for a manager who has made this level of commitment to their profession.

2)   Ask for total transparency in reporting. You might not want a report each month that is so technically detailed that it needs a translator (although one should be available if requested) but you should have basic metric information available to you upon request.   This should include: cost, impressions, cost per click, click through rate, cost per conversion and conversion rate. Some account managers will supply you with more detail on such issues as click fraud (good to know because an account manager watching this area in detail can request credits for invalid clicks) or a campaign change history that will detail how much work is being done in your account. Some account managers set-up accounts and then put them on a computer controlled "autopilot." The campaign change history is a good way to make sure this is not happening with your account.

3)   Before you start a paid advertising campaign your account manager should do a discovery profile of your business. The more the manager knows about your business the better that manager can customize your PPC account. Some basic questions they should be asking are:

- What is your value proposition?
- Who is your ideal customer?
- What times of the day, month, year are you the busiest?
- What is the transaction value of a new customer? Lifetime value of a new customer? What are you willing to pay to acquire a customer?

4) A good account manager will help you set budget goals that are realistic for your company at this time. More important, they will work with you to use profits from prior campaigns to build a marketing budget that is based on these profits and not draining working capital.

5) A good account manager will set realistic goals so that you will know if you are on target.

I began this chapter by pointing out how popular PPC advertising is in the roofing industry. I also said that far too often we see contractors who think about paid search engine advertising like an ad in the yellow pages--put it out there and wait to see what happens.

This is a costly error! PPC can be the single largest source of new business for your company, and the highest return on advertising investment you make. But only if you take the time to carefully monitor and manage your account. Don't let yourself get so busy that you ignore your PPC account. Better to pay a management fee for an effective and well managed account than to save a few dollars doing it yourself and then not doing it.

WHAT TO DO NOW:

1. Decide if Pay Per Click is a marketing channel for your business.

If yes, decide on the monthly investment you are willing to make in PPC advertising. As I said earlier, it is not uncommon for the cost per click to be $35 or more. That means to get 100 clicks in a month would be a $3500 investment.

2. If your intended monthly spend is going to be $1500 or more then I strongly encourage you to hire an experienced manager. Even with a relatively small monthly investment a qualified PPC account manager will pay for themselves in both campaign results and the time they save you.

It is common for a PPC manager to charge you a monthly fee plus a percentage of the ad spend. For smaller accounts the percentage may not be charged. You'll have to shop around. Use the criteria I suggested earlier in the chapter to interview account managers. If you talk with one of the large companies offering PPC services, WordStream or Bright Local for example, pay close attention to their agreements and how they are going to manage your account. Also, will you have a specific person assigned to be your point of contact, or will you be working with one of their "teams?"

3. If you choose to manage your PPC account "in house" then I have a report that you can download for free by going to this link:

http://bit.ly/2IJZo30

My report will give you a series of detailed checklists to follow as you create and manage your account. This will help you maximize your return on PPC ad campaigns.

Appreciation Marketing--Mining Past Customers for Referrals

The strategy I'm going to share with you in this chapter is perhaps the easiest, and most cost efficient, marketing program that I have used. It is a technique that is based on two concepts that are so well known that they are almost intuitive for a business owner:

1. it is less expensive to work with a past customer or their referrals than it is to go out and acquire a new customer, and

2. people like to feel appreciated, and will reward you with their referrals, when you express gratitude for their business.

While we all know these ideas to be true, how many of us actually take the time to stay in contact with our past clients? Other than thanking them at the conclusion of the job, what do you do to sustain the goodwill you created by doing a great job for them?

When I ask these questions to new clients the answer is usually, "well, nothing." Some send a thank you card through the mail, but not consistently to all customers. Others send an occasional email asking for referrals, but again not very consistently. Most do nothing, focusing their advertising budget on finding the next job.

That's a mistake, and I'm going to show you a system that can help you automate the process of staying in touch with past clients and creating consistent, top quality referrals from them.

First, let me share some statistics from the Direct Mail Marketing Association. They did an analysis of the methods that most businesses use to stay in contact with their customers, and the "open rate" of those efforts. That is, how many of their customers actually opened what they sent (that doesn't guarantee they read it, just opened.) You may find the data surprising.

1. Sending emails · · · · · · · · · · · · · · · · 15% get opened

2. An email sent to an "opt-in" list
(like a quarterly newsletter) · · · · · · 35% are opened

3. A letter in a business envelope · · · 45% open rate (people sort their mail over the trashcan)

4. A greeting card envelope · · · · · · · 94%!!! get opened

When someone receives what looks like a greeting card the odds that they will open and look at it are more than double what you can expect from other ways to communicate.

You're probably thinking something like, "great, I've bought boxes of thank you cards. They're sitting in a desk drawer because I'm too busy to sit down and write the message and get it into the mail." I have the same problem. Maybe you've tried what I used to do, have the sales team write thank you cards to their own prospects and customers. That worked...for about two weeks!

Ten years ago I solved this problem for my business. That's when one of my friends who also owns an advertising agency introduced me to a company called Send Out Cards. This is an internet based company that prints a custom greeting card and mails it for you. These are not electronic cards that come in an email, but an actual printed card that is delivered by the US mail. It is a service that is almost too good to be true, especially when you realize how inexpensive it is.

How The Send Out Cards (SOC) Platform Works

Here are the basic details for how this amazing system works.

1. Send Out Cards is totally "cloud" based. That means that once you set up a customer account with the company you will be able to access your account from any computer in the world, as long as you have an internet connection.

2. Within your SOC account you have two databases. One is a "contact manager" list of your customers, prospects, vendors...really anyone you might want to send a card to. I have family members and non-business friends in my contact manager. This is a very robust customer relationship manager that allows you to keep notes on each person on your list, track specific dates for that person, as well as categorize then into different groups that you define. Your data is totally secure.

3. The second database is the "card manager." Here you will find over 15,000 professionally designed greeting cards in more than 200 categories (by way of comparison, a typical Hallmark store has between 1700 and 2000 cards to choose from.) What really makes the SOC program unique is the fact that you can design your own cards, specific for your company, and have them printed and sent. You can send 1 card, or 1000.

4. You can choose to send a card in four different sizes. A standard postcard, a two panel card like you would buy at the store, a three panel card (almost like a brochure), and then a "big card" that is 8.2" x 11.5" when you really want to create an impression.

There is also an option to create a font that is your own handwriting, so you can send cards written just like you write. (Or, if your penmanship is as bad as mine, you have someone in your office create the font.)

5. In 2018 Send Out Cards revised their business model and made it even more "customer centric." There are four levels or types of accounts. The primary difference between these is the monthly commitment. The Basic account has no monthly investment requirement, while the Enhanced, Premium, and Enterprise accounts require a monthly spend but offset that with a variety of benefits.

Rather than give details here that might be out of date when you're reading this, let me encourage you to visit www.SendOutCards.com/IMS to get the most current information. (Full disclosure: this is an affiliate site. If you were to join the SOC program through this link we would be paid a referral fee.)

One of the best features of the Send Out Cards program, in my opinion, is the ability to customize a card with your company logo or your own photos. Think about that. You can create a custom, one-off greeting card using the SOC online card creation program, upload a photo and/or your logo, and add a message in your own handwriting. When you push the Send Card button you're done!

Send Out Cards then takes your card file, prints it, addresses the envelope, puts the card in, seals, stamps, and takes it to the post office. All this is done within 24 hours. You never have to leave your desk. Since this is a cloud based system you can enter orders any time of day and any day of the week.

6. To enhance the program even more, Send Out Cards has added the ability to send a gift along with your card. The last time I looked there were more than 200 gifts that could be sent. Quite a few of these are appropriate for a business to send to customers and associates.

7. Here's another great feature for business owners: the Campaign function. Essentially this allows you to create a card one time, then use it as often as you like, with each card being customized to the individual recipient. When you create a campaign you can use an "insert name" function that will automatically put the name of each person in the right place within the card.

You can also create multi-card campaigns. This means you can "touch" past clients several times a year automatically. Literally, you set up the campaign one time and then let it run. We have clients who create their card marketing for the year in January and an office person takes over from there, adding new customers. Since cards are so inexpensive, you can contact your past clients quarterly for less than $10 a year. In most cases, just one referral from one past customer will pay for your entire program for the year!

There are a dozen or more 'pre-built' campaigns you can purchase from Send Out Cards, or you can easily design your own. We have developed a variety of campaigns that we share with our clients using the platform.

How We Use The SOC System

Over the past ten years we have evolved to a very streamlined use of Send Out Cards in our own marketing. Here are some of the things we do:

- "Nice to meet you" card after any first time contact with a potential client or referral source. These are typically sent after a networking meeting.
- Thank you for just about any reason you can think of. So few people actually say "thank you" these days, we like to stand out from the crowd and this is a big part of that effort.
- Quarterly touch with all past clients. These are not "send us your referral" pleas. Our philosophy is to offer valuable business insights or interesting facts that make them stop and think for a moment. This keeps us not only "top of mind" but in their mind in a positive way.
- Personal use: birthdays, anniversaries, congratulations, etc. Often including a gift.
- Holiday cards. We do not send Christmas cards, so many companies do that no one really remembers who sent them a card. We send a patriotic card on the 4th of July and another card the week before Thanksgiving.

Here is How You Can "Test Drive" the SOC Platform

We have an affiliate link that you can go to and explore the Send Out Cards program and send a card to yourself to test the system. There is no cost to you to do this. That link is:

www.SendOutCards.com/IMS

As you look through the site you'll see that Send Out Cards offers a "Referral Partner" option for someone who wants to use the platform as an income generator. This is not a requirement, you can use the complete system as a customer by selecting one of the four account types.

WHAT TO DO NOW:

1. Follow the link above and look through the SOC system. There is a video tutorial that will introduce you to the various parts of the platform. Send a card to yourself. Pay particular attention to the campaign function, this is a great tool for business users.

2. To learn some additional ways you might use Send Out Cards in your business, here is a link to a report I've written entitled, "29 Ways to Use Appreciation Marketing in Your Roofing Business."

http://bit.ly/2KuMQdK

3. If you decide you want to utilize the SOC system, and become a customer through our Affiliate Link, I'll send you three of the campaigns we use. Once you have your customer number from Send Out Cards, send me an email with that number and I'll transfer the campaigns to your account. My email address is: Gordon@TheAlchemyConsultingGroup.com.

4. Whether you decide to use SOC or buy cards and manage your own system, I encourage you to begin an Appreciation Marketing Campaign.

Appreciation Marketing is too often overlooked by busy business owners, yet it can pay huge dividends in both goodwill and referrals.

The late Maya Angelou once said what I think best describes the value of adding an Appreciation Marketing component to your marketing. She noted, "I've learned that people will forget what you said, people will forget what you did, but people will never forget how you made the feel."

Gordon Van Wechel

The Five Forces Impacting Your Profits

Forgive me, but I have to start this chapter with something that looks a lot like math. It's an equation that is basic for all of us in business: Profit = Price - Cost.

Pretty simple, right? If we sell something for a dollar, and the sum of our product cost, labor cost, office and other overhead is 75 cents, then we have a profit of 25 cents. On one level that's true, but how do we consistently get to and maintain a healthy profit margin? That's the challenge presented by the five forces.

While you may not have thought of it this way, there are five outside forces that every company competes against for profit. It doesn't matter what industry, what vertical market you operate in, these five forces are arrayed against you. It is rare that a company is significantly affected by all five. Some industries really feel the impact of rivals, for others a low barrier to entry is the primary issue. But every one of us is impacted by one or more of these five forces.

Most roofing contractors are challenged by at least three of the five!

I first learned this method of analyzing the business environment several years ago from a book by Michael E. Porter, "Competitive Advantage: Creating and Sustaining Superior Performance." Mr. Porter is a professor at the Harvard School of Business and has written several books analyzing the business climate. He is quite readable for a college professor, and I recommend his book.

I want to step back for just a few pages and look at these five forces and define them for you. In the following chapter I'm going to suggest a way you can overcome each of them and increase your profits. The five forces are:

1. Direct Competitors
2. Powerful Suppliers
3. Powerful Buyers
4. Threat of Entry
5. Substitutes

For most roofing contractors the force that exerts the greatest influence is rivals--direct competitors. The normal ways a business deals with this challenge is to lower prices or increase the advertising budget or offer incentives; all ways that will impact profits by either reducing price or adding to cost.

Powerful suppliers might be the companies you purchase your materials from, but GAF, Owens Corning, CertainTeed and the others have the same competition issues you do. They can offer loyalty programs and incentives for volume purchasing, but at the end of the day their pricing stays relatively constant.

What about other suppliers you might buy from? If you have done any advertising online then you have used Google Adwords and/or Facebook to place ads. In the last 18 months you might have noticed Google has reduced the number of their paid ads on a page from fifteen or more to four. What happens when there are fewer spots available? The price goes up. Since Google controls 75% of the online search volume, if you want to have ads display you pay the higher price, and reduce profits.

Powerful buyers might be the least impactful of the five forces on the roofing industry, with the possible exception of commercial roofing companies. The large property management firms will frequently play one contractor against another to extract the best price. For those who deal with government buildings and contracts, the extra compliance issues can take more time and reduce profits.

Another way that powerful buyers can impact your profits is by demanding additional services.

The low barrier to entry in the roofing business affects everyone. In every community there are "Chuck with a truck" contractors who don't maintain offices, carry proper insurance, or provide warranties. They can easily underbid legitimate contractors who run a 'real' business, and frequently the homeowner is just looking to save a few bucks regardless of the risk.

Similar to the low barrier to entry is the threat of substitutes. That is, contractors using lower quality materials to reduce job cost and win more bids.

As you read through the five forces you could probably recall multiple times when one of them impacted a contract and cost you profits. In the next chapter I'm going to introduce you to a marketing channel that will help you combat each of them. Here's a quick preview.

Direct competitors: what if you could track prospects in your local market, on a daily basis, in real time? That is, identify those people who are looking for a roofing contractor. You can find them first, before another contractor, and start the conversation and build credibility and trust.

Powerful Suppliers: Most people think that Google and Facebook advertising works on a bid basis, the person who is willing to pay this highest price per click gets the best position on the page. This is not true. Both of these platforms actually work on what is called a "relevance engine." What that means is that their primary concern is that the ad they show is going to be relevant to the prospect who is searching. The search engines want to be sure that when their customer, the searcher, clicks on an ad they find valuable information that helps them in their information quest. If they do, then they will continue to come back and Google and Facebook can show them more ads.

If you show ads and do not get a high click through rate, then Google and Facebook will think your ad is not relevant and charge you more per click. But if you upload a list of highly targeted prospects, people who have already demonstrated that they are looking for what you sell, and then advertise to that group, since they are already interested in hearing from you, your relevance score will go up and your cost per click will go down.

This lower cost per click means it costs you less to acquire a new customer. It is an effective way to counteract the control of powerful suppliers, and increase your profits. Think back to the formula: Profit = Price - Cost.

Powerful Buyers: If you know all of the people who are in the market for a roofing contractor every week you are less susceptible to the whims of a powerful buyer. You don't have a limited number of prospects, your pipeline is full. If you only have a few prospects you are a lot more willing to let them dictate terms. It's like playing poker and you just have a few chips left...you play more cautiously hoping to preserve what you have.

It is the negotiating power of these buyers that sense and takes advantage of your urgency. This power goes away when they are just one of hundreds of prospects you have a direct link to.

Second, when you can start the conversation with these buyers early in their process, you have the opportunity to answer the questions in their mind about your ability to help them resolve their problem and prove they can trust you. You're not waiting until they have decided exactly what they want and are just looking for the cheapest price.

Threat of Entry: when you can begin the conversation with a prospect early in their research phase, help them understand their options and establish trust with them, you can more easily beat out the contractor who can only compete on price.

Substitutes: in a similar way, when you have the opportunity to share your company value proposition with a prospect you have a much better opportunity to capture their business.

Let me wrap up this discussion of the five forces that are competing for your profits by saying this. Every one of your prospects has a motivation, an outcome that they want to accomplish, they're looking for a solution that delivers a result they don't have.

You're the same way with your business. But I hope that now you realize that the challenge isn't just how do I be more profitable, it's how can I consistently beat the five forces that are arrayed against me and become more profitable. And the answer is, I need a better strategy, one that directly attacks the five forces.

In the next chapter I'm going to introduce you to People Based Marketing, the powerful strategy that I have been talking about.

People Based Marketing

What If You Could Identify, By Name, Exactly Who Is Looking For A New Roof In Your Town?

(Authors note: Throughout this book I have been describing strategies for growing your business that you can implement yourself. This chapter is different. The strategy I describe here, People Based Marketing, is based on new technology that is just now becoming available to small companies. Alchemy Consulting is one of just a handful of agencies nationally with access to this data. If you would like to learn more about this new marketing channel please contact us.)

Imagine you're at an NFL game, with 60,000 fans in the stands screaming for their favorite team. What if I told you there were 50 people in that crowd who owned a home and were looking for a roofing contractor to come inspect and provide a bid to replace their roof. Could you identify them? Not very likely!

Through people based marketing you would be able to know all 50 of these people, most by name, and have their contact information available to follow up with them personally. Now instead of spending thousands of dollars each month broadcasting to the entire stadium, you could target your message to those 50 prospects who are looking for your service. We call these "In-Market" shoppers. How is this possible? In just a minute I'll show you, but first, let's think about how you are probably finding new customers today.

What You're Probably Doing Now

Most roofing contractors follow a pretty similar path to marketing their business. They start with a website, and perhaps someone to do ongoing optimization of that site in an effort to achieve a rank on the first page or two of Google. This is often frustrating because it is difficult to measure a return on your monthly investment, and tracking how many customers actually visit your site is not always that accurate.

Then there is social media. For most of us this is a huge time suck, posting on Facebook or Instagram, keeping up with LinkedIn, to tweet or not to tweet...when you get right down to it, we don't have the time to manage social media when we're trying to run our business.

Not all marketing is on the internet. Flyers, yard signs, knocking on doors, billboards; these are tried and true methods to generate leads and potential jobs. Maybe not the most efficient, but they still work. A few use radio and television campaigns, with cable stations offering more targeted options, this can be quite effective.

More and more contractors are turning to paid ads, primarily Google Adwords, as a way to stay on page one. Here again it is not a simple solution. Building landing pages, testing headlines and ad copy, and trying to improve your Quality Score can be expensive if you outsource, and bewildering if you try to manage these campaigns in-house.

Marketing To The Haystack--Not The Needle

All of these marketing channels have one thing in common, and that is the problem. They are a broad based appeal for business that speaks the masses in the hope of attracting the attention of the 1% who are looking for a roofing contractor. So you spend a lot of money every month on people who have no need for or interest in your services! Your real prospect is the proverbial "needle in the haystack," but you have to blanket the whole haystack to try and find them.

People Based Marketing

That has all changed in the last few months with the advent of People Based Market (PBM). What is People Based Marketing? It is the ability to recognize, by name, exactly who you are marketing to. *It is knowing the needles buried within the haystack of your market area.*

How do we do this? By analyzing the shopping habits and decision making processes of 252 million Americans across 5 billion websites. We actually process over 15 billion pieces of data each and every day. Essentially we have a giant listening engine that allows us to build extremely accurate profiles of real people looking for real products and services every day.

We do this through "cookies," small files that are sent from a website and stored on a user's computer. In addition we buy data through publishers who collect it from their subscribers and vendors. This is completely compliant with all internet regulations and search engine terms of service. Since we follow this process we know that the results we get are real people. Internet bots do not buy things!

This kind of information collection has been prominent for at least the last decade. About 18 months ago **we created an algorithm that allows us to evaluate these massive amounts of consumer data in a conceptual way, identifying buyer patterns and not just**

transactions. When we identify an actual buyer of a product, a new roof for example, the algorithm allows us to go back through their search history for the previous weeks. When we do this analysis over thousands of buyers across the country, distinct patterns emerge. Said another way, *buyers leave a breadcrumb trail of what they do before they buy.*

We can use this behavioral approach to identify new the people coming into the market. As keyword searches are done, and websites navigated, we are able to pick this up, and narrow these searches down to a specific zip code.

This is proprietary technology, and not available through your SEO company.

As I have explained this to people, they frequently relate our process to retargeting. That is a reasonable analogy, as we use cookie data just as is done in a retargeting campaign. The differences are that the typical cookie expires in two to four weeks, ours last a full year as we are tracking real people. We are also using what is known as a "smart cookie." That enables us to monitor activity across billions of websites and using a proprietary "Identity Graph" we can recognize an individual person as they go from site to site. We can then attach the data to a real person when recording paid transactions.

Our platform provides a weekly update of the people who are looking for a roofing contractor in the zip codes that are in your service area. We can also access the personal information for the prospect through 3rd party vendors. Each week we give you a list that includes the new people "In-Market" and removes those who are no longer looking for service.

A variation of the program is "site visitor." Here we add the smart pixel to your website and provide you with a record of all the prospects that visit your company website. You will receive a file that identifies these people for follow up. This is a smaller data pool than the complete In Market program, and is available at a more modest monthly investment.

It is a fact that 100% of all purchases come from people who are "In-Market". That is, people who are exhibiting the exact behavior that all the other buyers have.

How Does This Compare with Traditional Marketing?

If you have used Facebook ads in the past, you try to use their targeting and demographics. They optimize for conversions with their pixel, but you can't make it optimize for actual sales. You pay whatever price they determine, you can only run ads on their network, and you don't know who you are actually marketing to. You cannot use real buyers to improve front end targeting.

A Google Adwords campaign starts with the keywords you want to be displayed for. You never know if the click you receive, assuming you get clicks, is the first one a prospect makes, or the one just before they buy. You pay high prices, roofing ads in most major markets in the US are at $35 per click or higher depending on the specific keyword. You have no idea who is clicking your ads, and there is not a way to use buyer data to improve front end targeting.

As ad prices go up, (and they will go up), you either have to spend more on ads or accept fewer leads.

Cold email marketing typically has an 8% to 12% open rate. If you have an excellent subject line, maybe as high as 15%. But here again you are sending out hundreds of emails to people who are in the 90% that are not looking for your service. With "In-Market" data you can focus on those prospects who are actually looking for roofing services.

Direct mail is an option as well when you have "In-Market" leads. You can send your company brochure immediately to people who will be the most receptive to the information. You can even have one of your sales team be "in the neighborhood" and drop it off.

To summarize, when you are working with "In-Market" data you can use multiple channels to reach those people who are actively looking for your service. Instead of "broadcast marketing" to everyone in the area, you can focus your ad budget where it will do the most good. In fact, most contractors see their add spend decrease as their ROI increases with more precise targeting.

Summary of the Technology

- ✓ We track keyword search and website visit behavior on 252 million Americans, using cookies across 5 billion websites. This is completely legal, publishers and users agree as a condition of using the website.
- ✓ With our vendor relationships we can connect that data to people who have purchased online, so we have real people to track. We use this to build the database of users.
- ✓ We can start with highly relevant prospects from their behavior, and then optimize for sales. We can onboard sales and see what behaviors they did before they bought and produce a list of people doing that right now. These are next buyers in your market.
- ✓ The weekly list that we provide can be loaded into any on or off line platform, with the best costs and optimized for customer sales.

✓ Build a relationship before you sell. You build a relationship online the same way you do in person, you start a conversation with your landing page. Think conversations, not campaigns; conversations create customers. We attract prospects from the channels (Facebook, Google, direct mail, email, etc) to a place in which to converse, thus nurture their trust.

A True Competitive Advantage

With our data you have a significant advantage over the other contractors in your market area. First, <u>as an In-Market customer you are the only contractor with access to the data</u>. As long as you continue your month to month subscription, you "own" the market area. If you are using the Site Visitor program then you will know those prospects who come to your website.

Second, our technology allows you to <u>operate at a lower cost</u>, you pay less to acquire your customers. Lower cost leads to higher profits.

Finally, <u>our team will manage the targeted marketing</u> to your "In-Market" prospects as a part of your data purchase. That means we will create landing pages, design the ads, script the copy, and all aspects of maximizing the use of the "In-Market" prospect data. You determine your monthly ad spend, and direct the addition of new channels at your option.

The Future is Here

For as long as I can remember, certainly going back to the 1970's when I started my first business, as business owners we identified our "ideal customer" demographically. We targeted neighborhoods with more expensive homes, we looked at household income and the cars people drove as indicators of who we wanted to target with our marketing dollars. This is still a valid method for identifying prospects, but doesn't go far enough, it doesn't give you a true competitive advancate.

Today we have the ability to identify our most likely customers by their online behavior. The sites they visit, the time spent on a site, the pages clicked, the forms filled out all are monitored. That data is sifted, sorted, analyzed, and sold to business in what has become a multi-billion dollar industry. As more data sensors are placed and the algorithms refined behavior based marketing will be the norm. In fact, many analysts say that as soon as 2020 we will have over a billion "sensors" monitoring our behavior, with that data available for sale.

WHAT TO DO NOW:

1. Don't take my word for this rapidly evolving marketing channel. Do a Google search for some of these topics and learn more about these innovations:

- Sensor based technology
- Consumer behavior based marketing
- People based marketing

Or pick up a copy of this recently published book on the subject: "Revealing the Invisible--How Our Hidden Behaviors Are Becoming the Most Valuable Commodity of the 21st Century"

2. If you'd like to discuss whether your company is a candidate for People Based Marketing call me directly at 505-720-2647.

The 11 Most Asked Questions About

Working With The Alchemy Consulting Group

1. So Who is The Alchemy Consulting Group?

Alchemy is a strategic marketing and business growth consulting firm started in 2010 by Jennine Michael and Gordon Van Wechel. It is an outgrowth of a consulting practice that Gordon first began in 2003. Between them, Jennine and Gordon have over 60 years of hands on experience as entrepreneurs, building and selling several businesses of their own. The same is true of all of our associate consultants, who are experienced business owners. That means we know what it's like to work 80 hours a week and "wear all the hats" in the business.

Unlike most ad agencies or more traditional consulting firms, Alchemy has created a menu of services, we call them "modules." These have been designed to provide our clients with specific solutions to their business growth challenges regardless of how long you might have been in business. Whether you are the owner of a new business just starting out, or have an established company looking to expand, we can offer tools and strategies to help you take the next step. The benefit to you is that we don't expect you to fit into our "marketing mold." We will be able to help you evaluate exactly what you need, and can afford, at this time in your business.

2. Why Do I Even Need a Consultant?

Every great sports star, business person, and superstar is

surrounded by coaches and advisors. As the world of business moves faster and gets more competitive, it can be difficult to keep up with the changes in your industry as well as the innovations in marketing and management. Having a business growth consultant is no longer a luxury; it's become a necessity.

If you're honest, you know that it is almost impossible to get an objective answer from yourself. That is not to say that you cannot survive in business without a consultant, but it's almost impossible to thrive.

A consultant can see the forest for the trees. A consultant will make you focus on the game, making you run more laps than you feel like. A consultant will tell it like it really is. A consultant will give you small pointers. A consultant will listen, and understand your pain. A consultant will help you remember the dreams you had when going into business...and help you get back on track to achieving them.

3. OK, so What is the First Step?

We'll ask you to complete our Marketing Audit. This is a series of questions, most of them are simple Yes/No answers, but there are several questions that will require a more detailed response. The purpose of the audit is to help you pinpoint areas of strength in your marketing now, and help identify those aspects of your plan that could use further work. A common experience of people participating in this exercise is a lot of ideas and excitement about what can be done to bring in more customers and profits. It will also prompt some questions about specific marketing tactics and how to implement them.

Once you have returned your audit, we'll schedule a time to meet together. This typically is a 60 to 90 minute conversation where we help you dig deeper into the level your company is performing at today, and where you'd like it to be in twelve months. It is also an opportunity for you to get to know us a little more, and see if working together makes sense. At the end of this meeting, at your request, we will prepare a proposal detailing our recommendations specific to your company, and the investment you will be making. You can then decide when you'd like to begin.

There is no charge for this initial meeting.

4. What Will You Do, and How Long Will it Take?

Just as every person is different, we believe each business is different. The plan that we suggest for your business will be based on the evaluation we make after reviewing your Marketing Audit and the conversation we have in the initial meeting. Which is to say that I cannot give you a specific idea of what we will do in your business, because we haven't designed your plan yet.

I can tell you that while about 80% of our strategic marketing focus today is online, we still incorporate traditional offline tools like direct mail and telephone marketing. We do that because they work. The particular mix of strategies for your company will depend on your goals, current situation, budget, competitive landscape, and personnel available to handle an influx of new customers.

Here's something else. Part of the Marketing Audit considers your current capacity. That is, how much more business can you handle well? It is no value to your business suddenly bring in 100 new clients when you only have the staff to properly serve 15 of them. We call this evaluating the "inside reality" of your company and is included in our modules.

As far as how long a typical program might take, we like to make commitments in 12 month increments. We don't try to lock someone in a contract saying that, but the plan we design for you will be based on a year of implementation.

If you've been in business for more than a few months you've already seen, and maybe even purchased, one or more so called "quick fixes." Most consultants want you to believe that they can solve your business growth problems in a few days. Our philosophy at Alchemy is that establishing a foundation for long term success in your business means not just scraping the surface with a few "Google secrets." We prefer to design a multi-channel marketing strategy that offers you controlled growth. That means implementing one or two modules initially, then, as they pay for themselves, adding more marketing. Over the course of a year, working together, we help you fully capitalize on current markets for your product/service, and extend the reach of your company into new areas.

5. How Do You Know This Will Work in My Industry?

Really simple. Our team of consultants are experts in sales, marketing, business development, management strategies, hiring key people, and evaluation of markets; just to name a few of their competencies. With more than 250 business building tactics in our arsenal you will quickly see how effective and powerful our modules are.

Add to this the fact that we have consulted with more than 300 companies in over 50 business categories and you can see that very likely that we have worked in a business that is the same or very similar to yours.

6. How Much Time and Money will This Cost Me?

The first couple of months your involvement in the processes will require more time. That might be review of copy or collateral materials, training your team in a new sales system, or regularly scheduled update meetings you'll have with one of our team members. The actual implementation of tactics, what we call the "back office fulfillment" duties, are all done by one of our groups of specialists. If part of your program calls for a revision of your website, the actual work will be done by our web builders. If you are doing a Real Time Bidding program, then another of our teams will handle the day to day details of that marketing channel for you.

As to the financial investment...well, nothing! That is if you look at it from the same perspective as we do. That's the difference between a cost and an investment. Everything we propose for your company is a true investment in your future. Not only will you create great results in your business, but you'll learn more than just marketing strategies. Working with our consultants will give you an education from experienced entrepreneurs you could never get in school, and this is knowledge that you can repeat over and over.

So you don't think I'm dodging the question, let me give you a range. We have clients who invest as little as $500 monthly and others who spend $10,000 a month. It will depend on your company, budget, short and long term growth goals, and how aggressively you want to pursue them.

7. Are There Any Guarantees?

Will all of your business goals be met by working with us? Maybe, or maybe not. We will never promise any specific result, nor can we guarantee that any of your goals will become a reality. The bottom line is we are your consultants, but it is still your business and it's up to you and your team to take the sales opportunities we bring you and convert those prospects to customers and eventually to raving fans of your business.

Only *you* can be fully accountable for your success. We guarantee to give you the best service we can, the benefit of all our experience and proven business growth strategies, and to encourage and even cajole you to reach for your goals. But at the end of the day it is your business.

Here is the guarantee that we do offer. When we work with you to design a strategic plan we'll define some clear goals that should be achieved within the first four months of working together. If they have not been achieved in that time period then we will continue to work with you at no charge until those goals have been met.

8. You're Based in Another City, How Does That Work?

You may have read Thomas Friedman's book from a few years ago called "The World Is Flat." His point was that with the communication tools available today business has truly become international. Even the shoe store down the street can have an ecommerce website or a store on eBay and sell to the whole world. Our business is living proof of that new reality: 80% of our clients live in another state. We regularly supply them with reports and updates via email, and schedule progress review conversations using phone or Skype.

Occasionally a client will want us to be at their location for a specific purpose, but generally that is an expense that you don't need to incur.

9. Do You Just Help With My Marketing?

While our primary focus is on marketing and business growth strategies, we'll help you in other areas too. For example, part of our Reputation Marketing module includes a training program helping your staff become more adept at customer service. I mentioned earlier the concept of the "inside reality" of your company, we'll help you identify operations within your business that can be improved.

We strongly believe in systems, the more you can implement systems in your business the better you can run your business instead of having it run you!

10. When is The Best Time to Get Started?

Yesterday. Really.

OK, right now, today; before you take another marketing step, waste another dollar, lose another sale, work another 70 hour week.

Far too many business people wait and see. They confuse activity with accomplishment and think that working harder will make it all better. Remember, what you know got you to where you are. To get to where you want to go you've got to make some changes and most likely learn something new.

There is no time like the present to get started on your dreams and goals.

11. How Do I Start?

Call us toll free at 877-978-2110 and ask for a Marketing Audit. You'll be connected with one of our consultants who will help you get started. We'll set up a time for an interview so we can learn about your business. Then we'll work with you to create a plan that helps you achieve your goals on a timeline that is affordable and makes sense for your business.

This may seem like a big job at the beginning, but with an Alchemy Consultant you'll have someone guiding you each step of the way.

Could You Profit From A Free, One Hour Flash Consultation Focused On Your Business?

I want to thank you for buying this book, and if you've found this page it means you probably even read most of it. Total Market Takeover® was written to help you identify the best marketing strategies for your roofing company. We created this process because that's what we do at The Alchemy Consulting Group, help our clients grow their companies to meet their goals.

Would you like to talk about your business? Whether you are launching a new marketing campaign or innovating your business, I'd like to offer you a free, one hour "flash consulting" session.

What that means is a very quick, 10,000 foot view of your company and current marketing efforts. We'll ask a lot of questions, and answer yours. We might point you in a new direction, suggest a strategy that you hadn't considered, or help you look at what you're now doing in a new light.

This is a conversation about marketing and your business...it is not a thinly disguised pitch for you to hire us. Never once have I had anyone say it wasn't worth their time!

To take advantage of this offer you have to do a couple of things:

1. Enter this link into a browser window: http://bit.ly/2tPw9iS

2. Answer the questions, give me your contact info, and follow the instructions to fax or scan and email the report to us

3. I'll call and schedule an hour that works for both of us to meet by telephone

4. Come to our meeting with an open mind, a pen and pad ready

to take notes, and be in a quiet place where you will not be interrupted.

I look forward to talking with you.

Gordon

About the Author

Gordon Van Wechel is an entrepreneur who has built three national companies, each in a different industry. He has written six previous books, two of which became Amazon top sellers, and has been cited by all four of the major television networks as an expert in business marketing.

Gordon is a frequent speaker to business groups, and he teaches a marketing class to new business owners on behalf of the Service Corps of Retired Executives division of the Small Business Administration.

In addition to his own enterprises, he has travelled extensively in Asia, Africa, and the Middle East on behalf of several non-governmental organizations. His work there has focused on micro-enterprise programs that, to date, have resulted in the creation of over five hundred successful businesses, seventeen village schools, and numerous community development projects.

He is the founder and President of The Alchemy Consulting Group, a national marketing strategy and business-growth firm started in 2003 and based in Albuquerque, NM.